The Institute of Pacific Relations
ASIAN SCHOLARS AND AMERICAN POLITICS

The Institute of Pacific Relations.

ASIAN SCHOLARS AND AMERICAN POLITICS

By John N. Thomas

Seattle and London
UNIVERSITY OF WASHINGTON PRESS

This book was published with the assistance of a grant from the
Andrew W. Mellon Foundation.

Library of Congress Cataloging in Publication Data

Thomas, John N   1938-
    The Institute of Pacific Relations.

    Bibliography: p.
    1. Institute of Pacific Relations. 2. United States—Foreign relations
—East (Far East) 3. East (Far East)—Foreign relations—United
States. 4. United States—Politics and government—1953-1961. I. Title.
DU1.T46   327'.06'373   73-15504
ISBN 0-295-95294-6

TO SALLY, WITH LOVE

Preface

DESPITE the intentions of its founders, the Institute of Pacific Relations did not long remain a noncontroversial meeting ground for the peoples of East and West. Because of unexpected developments both in Asia and in America, and partly because of its own leadership, the IPR developed a significance greater than itself. By the mid-1950's, the IPR had become for some a victim of "McCarthyism"; for others, especially those keenly disappointed with events in Asia, it was a symbol of betrayal in foreign policy and cooperation with communism.

In undertaking this study of the IPR, I have chosen not to write a history of the organization as such. Rather, I have attempted to point out and discuss those issues which brought the institute into conflict first with itself and finally with political forces in America. Inevitably, such a discussion highlights some of the rough spots of IPR history while neglecting instances of day-to-day achievements. The hard work and devotion of many individuals to the institute, the camaraderie and excitement of its first two decades, and its solid contributions to Asian studies in America may thus seem slighted. For this I can only express a sense of regret as well as hope that this work may encourage others to address that task.

Foreign policy, while not the primary focus of this study, nevertheless was intertwined with the development of the

IPR. Both the Sino-Japanese conflict and the civil war in China had profound implications for the leaders and members of the institute. In later times the conflict in Indo-China placed significant new pressures on the Asian studies field. In this work I have attempted to provide just enough data on foreign policy matters to indicate the context in which Asian specialists were operating. I have avoided detailed discussion or analysis of the foreign policy issues themselves.

Many persons have aided the completion of this work. I would like to express particular thanks to Professors Allan Cole and Ruhl Bartlett of the Fletcher School of Law and Diplomacy, Tufts University, for their helpful comments and kind consideration during both the research and writing stages. I also wish to thank Professor Roy Young, chairman of the Department of Political Science, San Jose State University, for encouraging my research during the past year.

Thanks are also extended to Mrs. Kathryn Marlatt of San Jose State University for unfailingly fast and accurate typing assistance; to Columbia University Libraries for allowing me to examine their substantial collection of IPR documents; to the directors of the library of the University of British Columbia for permission to review institute documents retained in Vancouver; to the Hoover Institution Library for granting me access to the records of the San Francisco IPR; to the University of California Libraries for allowing me to examine the papers of two institute leaders.

Finally, I wish to express my appreciation to the numerous individuals who granted me personal interviews concerning various aspects of the IPR. In many cases their comments were invaluable in clarifying issues only touched on in written materials.

The author, of course, assumes responsibility for the facts and interpretations presented in this work.

J.N.T.

June 1973

Contents

The Institute of Pacific Relations
ASIAN SCHOLARS AND AMERICAN POLITICS

1

The Adventure Begins

ON the founding, but only the founding, there is no dispute.
The Institute of Pacific Relations (IPR) was born in Honolulu,
Hawaii, in 1925 at a meeting organized by a number of people
associated with the YMCA movement in Hawaii. Frank
Atherton, a Honolulu businessman, Merle Davis of the
YMCA, and Ray Lyman Wilbur, president of Stanford
University, were prominent among the organizers.[1] They
and many others hoped that American understanding of
Asia could be improved by international application of the
YMCA idea of bringing leaders of different racial commu-
nities together for frank discussions of differences.

The concept quickly took hold. The participants at Honolulu,
enthusiastic about the possibilities of such meetings, thought
that a permanent body was necessary. It was agreed that a
permanent secretariat would be established and that the
delegates would meet again in Honolulu two years later
to establish an Institute of Pacific Relations.

By the time of the second conference in 1927, six national
councils (the United States, Canada, Australia, New Zea-
land, China, and Japan) had been established.[2] Represent-

1. John B. Condliffe, "The IPR," undated memorandum. I wish to
express my appreciation to Dr. Condliffe for allowing me to examine
this memorandum.

2. *Problems of the Pacific, Proceedings of the Second Conference of
Institute of Pacific Relations* (Chicago: University of Chicago Press,
1928), p. VI.

atives also attended from the United Kingdom, Korea, and the Philippines. The delegates adopted a constitution saying the IPR had been set up to "study the conditions of the Pacific peoples with a view to the improvement of their mutual relations."[3] A Pacific Council composed of represent-atives of the member councils was to be the chief executive organ of the International IPR; a secretary-general and a small staff—termed the secretariat—were assigned the task of carrying out the institute's day-to-day activities. Among the chief committees established were those dealing with finance, research, education, and publications.

Funds for the Pacific Council were to be secured from each national council, individuals, foundations, and business organizations. Each member council was expected to be self-supporting. The American Council, later called the American Institute of Pacific Relations, was the largest and best funded national council. From the beginning it exerted a strong influence over the International IPR.

Reporting on the second international conference, Merle Davis, the first secretary-general, termed the IPR "non-sectarian, non-controversial, and non-propagandist."[4] This undoubtedly represented the hope of the early IPR leaders as well as many of the delegates at Honolulu. They saw the IPR primarily as a means of crosscultural contact and exchange of individual views in a private framework.

Not all the participants at Honolulu held to such a restrictive view of the IPR, however. British delegate Sir Frederick Whyte injected a highly political note by using his private discussions with Chinese delegate David Yui for what amounted to semiofficial Sino-British negotiations. After each session, cables would be sent to the respective foreign offices reporting on the day's events and requesting instructions for future meetings.[5]

Far more important for the future of the institute was the attitude of Edward C. Carter, secretary of the American Council of the IPR. A veteran of the YMCA movement, Carter joined the IPR in 1926 and made it his life for twenty-

3. Ibid.
4. Ibid.
5. Condliffe, "The IPR," p. 17.

three years. Handsome, free-wheeling, impulsive, and ambitious, Carter was a whirlwind of activity for the IPR and a constant source of ideas for new programs. In his personality and programs he carried the seeds both of the IPR's fame and of its destruction.

Carter very quickly demonstrated his impatience with what he must have considered the limited vision of the IPR's founders. A strong believer in the notion that even the hottest international issues of the day could benefit from debate by private persons, Carter believed that IPR conferences should not avoid discussion of current political questions. He also foresaw a vastly expanded IPR role in a then largely underdeveloped field—Asian research. With great energy and enthusiasm, although not always with adequate consultation with the American Council or International IPR research committees, Carter pressed New York foundations with proposals for new IPR research projects.

By 1927 Carter succeeded in convincing Secretary-General Merle Davis and the Pacific Council that a large increase in staff was necessary to carry out adequate research on the Far East. The secretary-general accepted Carter's proposal that Davis should concentrate on organizational matters such as the formation of new IPR councils, while Carter secured the necessary funds via his foundation contacts.[6]

During 1929 both personal and philosophical frictions between Carter and Davis widened as the IPR's third conference at Kyoto loomed closer. A portion of the funds promised by Carter had not been secured, and it seemed clear that Davis would have to inform the conference of a substantial deficit in IPR accounts; in addition, a letter from Carter to Charles Loomis, an aide to Davis, was sent in error to another staff member. The letter made it apparent that Loomis was acting as Carter's agent in an effort to displace Davis. The letter was shown to Davis, who discussed the matter with Frank Atherton and eventually Loomis; however, Loomis was retained. Davis did warn the new IPR chairman, Jerome Greene, about Carter, but Greene replied

6. Ibid., p. 21.

that he had to get seven or eight hours of sleep per night and could not watch Carter for twenty-four.[7]

As the meeting approached, it became increasingly clear that Davis' position was untenable. Seemingly unable or unwilling to resist trends which he disliked, Davis resigned, expressing his disagreement with what he termed a trend away from the early IPR concentration on cultural and economic problems toward a new emphasis on the study of political conflict in the Far East. Davis thought that the IPR conferences had felt the weight of this change, reflected in the fact that the original purpose of individual, frank exchange of views was being replaced by group opinions.[8] Loomis was chosen as acting secretary-general, but the real leadership in the IPR was now in New York with Edward C. Carter. Two years later at the Banff Conference, Carter was appointed secretary-general.

Some of the proceedings at Kyoto seemed to bear out Davis' concern about increasing IPR involvement in controversial political matters. But this time the source of controversy was not British, but Chinese. Hoping to obtain a sympathetic ear for their case against Japanese activities in Manchuria, the Chinese delegates circulated copies of the "Tanaka Memorial," which allegedly outlined Japan's expansionist desires. The Japanese, who were anxious to avoid any discussion of Manchuria at Kyoto, termed the document a forgery.[9] Finally, the Pacific Council was able to convince the Chinese to withdraw it.[10]

THE MOVE TO NEW YORK

As important changes go, the movement of the IPR from Honolulu to New York was accomplished with a minimum of

7. John B. Condliffe, "The Kyoto Conference," undated memorandum, p. 10

8. Resignation letter of J. Merle Davis, July 18, 1930; from the IPR files located at the Special Collections Division, Columbia University Library, New York (hereafter cited as Columbia Files).

9. Further examination by historians suggests that the Japanese were accurate in calling the document a forgery. See Franz H. Michael and George E. Taylor, *The Far East in the Modern World* (New York: Holt, Rinehart and Winston, 1964), p. 542.

10. Condliffe, "The Kyoto Conference," p. 16.

apparent fuss. But beneath the surface were frictions and disagreements over fundamental goals which remained unresolved. International IPR Research Secretary John B. Condliffe and Carter differed over the nature of IPR research. Condliffe thought it should stress long-range factors, particularly the fundamental economic conditions affecting current problems; Carter wanted more stress on current issues themselves. Unable to resolve the dispute, Condliffe resigned.

Two early IPR leaders were also uneasy about the shift. Ray Lyman Wilbur saw an early cleavage between the "cultural" emphasis of many West Coast IPR members and the "political" orientation of some members of the New York office.[11] Frank Atherton was concerned that Carter's appointment would lead to a New York orientation for the IPR. He urged that Carter spend at least one-half to one-third of his time in Hawaii.[12] In spite of their qualms, both men remained in the IPR and gave it their support.

By dint of his own drive and the staunch cooperation of numerous individuals as well as his ability to obtain substantial foundation and corporate assistance, Carter was able to forge the IPR into *the* organization for the study of Eastern Asia, both as an American group and as a fledgling private international body. National councils were added from France, Great Britain, and the USSR. The major journals of the International IPR and the American Council, *Pacific Affairs* and *Far Eastern Survey*, were consulted widely by scholars and bureaucrats alike. IPR grants provided a major boost to Asian scholarship and impressive numbers of IPR-assisted books began to roll off the presses. The benefit for Asian studies is especially large when it is recalled that during the 1930's the commercial press was far less interested in Asia than it is today, and that university presses and Asian studies centers were generally in stages of infancy.[13]

11. Edgar Robinson and Paul Edwards, eds., *The Memoirs of Ray Lyman Wilbur* (Stanford, Calif.: Stanford University Press, 1960), p. 608.

12. Atherton to Newton D. Baker, May 6, 1933, Columbia Files.

13. The research committees of the Pacific Council and the American Council were responsible for the bulk of the book publishing conducted by the IPR. Generally, the IPR assisted with grants at the research

By the mid-1930's Carter had attracted an able and loyal staff which was to make a heavy imprint on both the International Secretariat and the American Council. The most important of these recruits were Owen Lattimore, editor of *Pacific Affairs* (1933-41), Frederick V. Field, secretary of the American Council (1934-40), and William L. Holland, international research secretary and later Carter's replacement as secretary-general.

Owen Lattimore, although an American and a professor, was by no means a typical product of American academe. Born in the United States, he was taken to China at an early age by his father. Young Owen studied in English and Swiss schools, but left college before obtaining his degree in order to see first-hand conditions in the area which most interested him—the inner Asian frontiers of China. By means of personal travel and residence and the mastery of several languages, including Chinese, Mongolian, and Russian, Lattimore gained expertise in an area little known to Western scholars. After many years' residence in Asia, he returned to the United States to seek positions in teaching and research. It was at this point that Carter persuaded him to become editor of *Pacific Affairs* on a half-time basis.

Lattimore brought to the IPR an inquiring mind, an enjoyment of intellectual controversy, and a penchant toward wide-sweeping historical analysis and synthesis. He also brought some strong views on American, Soviet, and Japanese policies in the Far East, which he disseminated widely in a prolific career of lecturing and writing. Lattimore's personality and views, combined with the combustible situation in the Far East during the 1930's, insured that the IPR would not be the "non-controversial" organization which Merle Davis had hailed in 1927.

Frederick Vanderbilt Field was cut from far different cloth, but ultimately no less a source of controversy for the IPR. Field was born into wealth as the son of William Field and Lila Vanderbilt Sloane, granddaughter of Commodore Cornelius Vanderbilt.[14] Field was hired by

---

stage and secured publication through a commercial press.

14. Julian Maxwell, "Frederick Vanderbilt Field," *American Mercury*, 75 (November 1952): 31.

Edward Carter in 1928 after education at Harvard and the London School of Economics. Although a member of the Harvard *Crimson* staff, Field was not known as a political activist in Cambridge. One college aneodote, however, may shed some light on Field's reaction to great wealth and provide some clue to his later political evolution. The writer, Lucius Beebe, has described an elegant dinner at Locke-Ober's in Boston during Field's college days. In the middle of the meal Field rushed out into the snow and offered a dirty-faced newsboy fifty cents to press his nose against the window and look hungry so that the guests would be properly ashamed of their affluence.[15]

Personable, hard-working, and a flexible administrator, Field was held in high esteem by his colleagues during his tenure as secretary of the American Council (1934-40). What later tarnished his image, and that of the IPR, was an increasingly leftward political metamorphosis culminating in Field's open identification with Communist causes by the mid-1940's.

The exact course of Frederick Field's evolution toward communism is still obscure. That Field was at least quite familiar with Communist activities by 1933 seems evident in this memorandum which he sent to a member of the American Council staff: "To come to the point, Harris is, between you and me, a member of the CP, and this affair in Chicago is of course a thoroughly radical meeting. What he wants is someone to give the unadulterated dirt on rural conditions in China, not from any expert and academic point of view, but from what I believe is known as the 'human approach.' "[16]

By 1935 Field had joined the editorial board of the Communist-controlled journal, *China Today*, under the pseudonym of Lawrence Hearn.[17] According to later testimony by Whittaker Chambers, by 1937 Field had become a member of the Communist underground.[18]

15. *Newsweek*, 35 (May 15, 1950), 28-30.

16. Field to Harriet L. Moore, November 6, 1933, Columbia Files.

17. Philip Jaffe to the author, September 15, 1970. Jaffe states that non-Communists were among both the editors and contributors to *China Today* during the late 1930's.

18. In his writings, Chambers says that in 1937 he utilized Field in

After his resignation as secretary (but not as trustee) of the American Council in 1940, Field's leftward migration became much more apparent. As secretary of the leftist American Peace Mobilization, Field supervised allegedly pacifist demonstrators picketing the White House against possible United States involvement in the European war. After the Nazi invasion of Russia, however, the pickets were withdrawn virtually overnight.[19] By 1943 Field was a correspondent for the *Daily Worker* and by 1945 a contributor to the Communist theoretical journal, *Political Affairs*. By the early 1950's he was well known in the popular press as the "financial angel" of numerous Communist front groups.[20]

William L. Holland had neither the personal flamboyance of Owen Lattimore nor the political leftism of Frederick Field. What he did offer was a keen mind and a strong sense of devotion to his work, both of which he displayed in abundance during more than three decades of service to the IPR. Holland began his IPR career as a research assistant in the International Secretariat, became research secretary in 1933 and finally secretary-general in 1946. A New Zealander who became an American citizen only during the mid-1940's, Holland is the first to admit his early unfamiliarity with American politics.[21] Perhaps because of this initial political naïvete and certainly because of his personal flexibility, Holland eventually became the most improtant IPR leader who retained the confidence of the diverse elements within the institute.

The staffs of the International IPR and the American Council, both housed in the same building in New York,

---

an effort to recruit State Department employee Lawrence Duggan for the Communist party. See Whittaker Chambers, *Witness* (New York: Random House, 1952), p. 382. At Senate hearings in 1951, Chambers testified that J. Peters, an important Communist official, told him that Field was a member of an underground unit of the party. See U.S., Congress, Senate, Committee on the Judiciary, Subcommittee on Internal Security, *Hearings on the Institute of Pacific Relations*, 82d Cong., 2d sess., 1951-52, p. 490 (hereafter cited as *McCarran Hearings*.).

19. Richard L. Williams, "The Reds' Pet Blueblood," *Life*, 31 (July 23, 1951): 40.

20. Ibid., p. 36.

21. William L. Holland, personal interview, March 9, 1970.

also made a significant impact on the IPR. Generally young, idealistic, individualistic "liberals" of the thirties,[22] the staff was attracted by the enthusiasm and relatively unstructured atmosphere for creativity which the IPR offered at that time. Although membership on the staff changed often, several deserve mention at this point: Harriet Moore, Catherine Porter, Miriam Farley, Bruno Lasker, Kathleen Barnes, and Russell Shiman.

All organizations must make difficult decisions about their purposes and the principal means of achieving them. By 1930. the IPR had in effect decided to expand the relatively restricted vision of the organization held by several of its founders. But events in both the Far East and in America forced upon the organization decisions regarding several additional dilemmas having important implications for the nature of the organization and its ability to survive subsequent changes in the American political climate. Among these questions were the role of the Soviet Council in the IPR, the Sino-Japanese War, the growth of Chinese communism, and the United States entry into World War II.

FORMATION OF THE SOVIET COUNCIL

At the second Honolulu Conference in 1927, the Pacific Council authorized Secretary General Merle Davis to explore the possibilities of Soviet participation in the IPR. Shortly after the conference in 1927, Davis traveled to Moscow where he met with Soviet Asian specialists and explained the aims of the IPR.[23] Davis' initiative did not bear immediate fruit, however, and the job of securing Soviet entry was left to Edward Carter. A strong believer that even the deepest differences of opinion would benefit from private discussion and debate, Carter made every effort to get and keep Soviet participation in the IPR.

In 1930 Carter requested International IPR Research Secretary J. B. Condliffe to pass through Moscow and assess Soviet willingness to enter the IPR. Condliffe obtained an

22. Dorothy Borg, personal interview, May 9, 1963.
23. American IPR (hereafter AIPR), *Commentary on the McCarran Report on the IPR* (New York, 1953), p. 7.

audience with Foreign Minister Maxim Litvinoff, who informed him that the Soviets had no objections to forming a group.[24] A group was set up the next year but did not apply for IPR membership. It was not until three years later, after the establishment of Soviet-American diplomatic relations and a personal visit from Carter, that Moscow decided to join. In retrospect it seems likely that the Soviets were somewhat suspicious about the benefits of joining a "bourgeois" institution funded by "monoply capitalists" such as the Rockefeller Foundation.

Both Carter and Lattimore were intrigued by the prospects of significant Soviet participation in the IPR. Carter at one point thought that the involvement of the Soviet Council would have a large impact on the IPR's work.[25] Lattimore hoped that Soviet authors would make frequent contributions to *Pacific Affairs*. IPR staff members Joseph Barnes and Harriet Moore, both Soviet specialists, hoped to obtain documentary Soviet materials for the IPR library.

Such high hopes were not to be fulfilled. With much fanfare from Carter, the Soviets did attend one IPR conference at Yosemite in 1936. One Soviet article was submitted to *Pacific Affairs* and exchange of research materials was begun. After 1938, however, even this meager level of Soviet participation was not maintained. The Soviets attended no further conferences and submitted no additional articles. Even routine IPR correspondence went unanswered by the Soviet Council.[26] With the benefit of hindsight, it seems most likely that Soviet participation was first hindered and finally terminated by the extensive Stalinist purges which increasingly affected Soviet scholars during the 1930's. Ultimately, some Soviet IPR leaders did not survive the purges.[27] By the late thirties, given the nature of Soviet domestic politics, it

24. Condliffe to Benjamin Mandel, September 18, 1951, from the papers of John B. Condliffe, Bancroft Library, University of California, Berkeley, California (hereafter cited as Condliffe Papers).

25. Carter to Escott Reid, February 10, 1935, Columbia Files.

26. William L. Holland, personal interview, March 18, 1970. The single Soviet article submitted was accepted; see A. J. Kantorovich, "The Sale of the Chinese Eastern Railway," *Pacific Affairs*, 8 (December 1935): 397-408.

27. William L. Holland, personal interview, March 18, 1970.

would not have been illogical for officials of the Soviet Council to avoid further contacts with Western-dominated groups such as the IPR.

Even this very short and marginal Soviet participation was to pose some difficult choices for IPR leaders and to shed some light on the extent of their willingness to placate Soviet suspicions. Edward Carter, for example, told the Russians in 1934 that "the bourgeois liberal philosophy might very possibly be false but it was in any case the most effective program for the Institute to work at the present moment and . . . afforded a substantial medium for Soviet participation.[28]

Owen Lattimore was deeply disappointed by the first (and only) Soviet contribution to *Pacific Affairs*. He considered it "rank propaganda" and "an uncomfortable wallop in the midriff" to his expectations about Soviet Far Eastern scholarship.[29] But Lattimore continued to give Soviet books generally favorable reviews in *Pacific Affairs*.

Not all IPR writers were as favorable to the Soviets, however, and Lattimore bore the brunt of occasional fierce criticism from the Soviet Council. The chairman of the Soviet IPR, V. E. Motylev, wrote Lattimore in 1935 to protest strongly against an article by William Henry Chamberlin, whom he called an "anti-Soviet libeller."[30] Three years later Motylev wrote to express his relief that a proposed article by L. M. Hubbard had not yet appeared in *Pacific Affairs*. Lattimore's solution was to edit out one paragraph which he thought was the most objectionable to the Soviets and to ask for a rejoinder from the Soviet Council.[31]

A far more nettlesome question was the attitude that IPR

28. "Report of a Conversation at a Tea Given to Mr. Carter, Secretary General of the Institute of Pacific Relations, at the Hotel National on May 28, 1934, by the Research Workers of the Communist Academy," Columbia Files.

29. *Commentary on the McCarran Report on the IPR*, p. 7.

30. V. E. Motylev to Owen Lattimore, January 15, 1938, Columbia Files.

31. Lattimore to G. E. Hubbard, February 8, 1938, Columbia Files. For a further discussion of Soviet criticism of *Pacific Affairs*, see below in this chapter.

officials should take toward an issue dividing the American intellectual community during the 1930's—the Soviet purge trials. Both Field and Carter accepted the Soviet version of the trials—that those charged were part of a "fascist" plot to overthrow the Soviet government. Both were concerned over the adverse image of the Soviet Union which the trials had created in the Western press.

Carter thought that the American Council was in a good position to handle the matter.[32] In his own capacity he wrote to a number of people who were perplexed about the trials and sent them copies of the verbatim Soviet report of the proceedings. He also wrote radio commentator Mary Van Kleeck, who had described the trials as a "victory over fascism." Carter acclaimed her view as "far and away the best brief analysis of the recent trials that I have seen."[33] Field, however, was more circumspect. He parried Carter's suggestion that the American IPR take an active role, saying that it did not have jurisdiction in that area.[34] Instead, he urged an officer of the American-Russian Institute to undertake the job of correcting the "false impressions" about the purge trials conveyed in the United States press.[35]

As editor of *Pacific Affairs*, Owen Lattimore was in a somewhat more delicate position. He ran no articles on the trials, but finally felt the need to reply when William Henry Chamberlin wrote in to urge that readers use great caution in accepting the official Soviet explanation for the proceedings. Lattimore followed Chamberlin's commentary with his own, which contended that the trials would aid "democracy" by giving the average Soviet citizen more ground to protest if victimized in the future by government officials.[36]

It is easy, of course, to pick out instances in which IPR officials showed favoritism to the Soviet Council. There are no doubt many occasions on which the IPR demonstrated considerable sensitivity to the interests of other national councils, especially those of China and Japan. However, it

32. Carter to Field, March 8, 1937, Columbia Files.
33. Carter to Van Kleeck, March 28, 1938, Columbia Files.
34. Field to Carter, March 9, 1937, Columbia Files.
35. Field to Virginia Burdich, March 9, 1937, Columbia Files.
36. *Pacific Affairs*, 11 (September 1938): 371-72.

is hard to examine the record of IPR contacts with the Soviets without concluding that several high institute officials were overly optimistic about the prospects for Soviet participation and were especially sensitive to Soviet concerns about the treatment of the USSR in IPR journals. Had the Soviets taken up the suggestion to take a significant part in IPR activities, it seems likely that some serious internal discussion of this role might have taken place. As has been noted, however, the Soviets for their own reasons chose to play only the most minimal role. Only later, and from a radically different perspective, were questions of the role of the Soviet Council to be revived.

IPR PUBLICATIONS DURING A TIME OF TURMOIL

As previously noted, the ascendancy of Edward Carter to the post of secretary-general meant in effect that the IPR had decided to deal with current political controversies in the Far East. Exactly how this decision would be reflected in IPR publications, however, was not determined. Two significant developments in Asia forced a decision of sorts: the Sino-Japanese War and the growth of the Chinese Communist movement.

Pacific Affairs

When Owen Lattimore became editor of *Pacific Affairs* in 1933 he inherited a relatively noncontroversial publication which had attempted rather gingerly to discuss Far Eastern political matters. Lattimore himself had no qualms about the issue. He believed that *Pacific Affairs* could not avoid the controversial questions of the day.[37]

By 1936 Lattimore had succeeded in turning *Pacific Affairs* into a lively quarterly of factual information and diverse views. A comment and opinion section introduced in 1935 had begun to produce a smattering of the intellectual debate which he richly enjoyed. Lattimore provided additional variety to his readers by including occasional analyses by unconventional writers such as Harold Isaacs, who provided

37. Institute of Pacific Relations, *Report of the International Secretariat to the Pacific Council*, 1933-36 (New York, 1936), p. 77.

a Trotskyite view of events in China for the September 1935 issue.[38]

These innovations, however, were achieved only at a price of greater friction among the various IPR national councils. Controversial articles about China and Japan inevitably drew anguished criticism from the editorial correspondents of the Chinese and Japanese councils, who were allowed to examine articles prior to publication. The lack of thoroughly defined procedures for resolving such disputes constantly placed the editor in a delicate situation.

It was to alleviate this situation that Lattimore presented the Pacific Council with a fundamental issue for decision. Reporting to the Yosemite Conference (1936) on the development of *Pacific Affairs*, Lattimore called for a clarification of the nature of the journal. Should it be essentially an organ devoted to papers contributed by the various national councils, with each having veto power over the final product? Or should it be an independent organ of free expression, similar to Western academic journals? Lattimore clearly preferred the latter, but he implored the Pacific Council, as the executive organ of the International IPR, to make the choice.[39]

As so often happened in the IPR, no decision was made. The Pacific Council deferred action on Lattimore's proposal. No instructions were issued then or later, although Lattimore again brought up his proposal two years later. The failure of the Pacific Council to act demonstrated its inability to provide adequate leadership and placed primary responsibility in the hands of the staff. In effect, Lattimore was told to make the best of the situation without firm instructions.

The result was that Lattimore continued to implement a number of his own plans to further vitalize *Pacific Affairs*. He continued to publish articles on controversial Asian political questions, sometimes by authors Lattimore himself characterized as "left-wing," despite the friction he knew would result among the national councils.

38. See Harold Isaacs, "Perspectives of the Chinese Revolution: A Marxist View," *Pacific Affairs*, 7 (September 1935): 269-83

39. IPR, *Report of the International Secretariat to the Pacific Council*, 1933-36, p. 78.

Lattimore considered but finally dropped a more controversial idea: that *Pacific Affairs* adopt a distinct editorial point of view about Far Eastern questions. In his 1936 report to the Pacific Council, Lattimore included the curious comment that, because of the nature of the IPR's structure, he had been unable to "maintain the kind of consistency or continuity which results in building up, number by number, an unvarying point of view, or the kind of advance along a constructive line of thinking which results from the coordinated decisions of a unanimous group."[40]

It can be questioned whether the editor of an objective academic journal, much less that of a journal such as *Pacific Affairs*, should seek the goal suggested by Lattimore. It can be argued that such tactics should have been employed only by a journal of opinion that made no bones about its editorial proclivities. But Lattimore's thinking was strongly influenced by his increasing concern with Japanese policies in the Far East. One of the first American writers to sound warnings of Japanese intentions in China,[41] Lattimore was an early exponent of collective security against Japan. The main question was whether or not to manifest such feelings in *Pacific Affairs*. With the Marco Polo Bridge incident of July 7, 1937, and the beginning of undeclared Sino-Japanese war, the pressures to speak out increased.

Lattimore's was not the only voice calling on the IPR to support collective security. In 1936 a member of the Soviet Council told IPR leaders that the main problem of *Pacific Affairs* was its lack of a general line. It should, he asserted, show that collective security was the only way to peace. Edward Carter replied that there was disagreement within the organization whether this was a legitimate function of the IPR. Lattimore told the Soviets that he personally was willing to adopt a line favoring collective security but that he could not dictate to the other councils. Any movement toward such a policy would have to be stimulated by contributions. The next year, Lattimore relied on the same line of reasoning

40. Ibid., p. 80

41. See Owen Lattimore, *Manchuria: Cradle of Conflict* (New York: Macmillan, 1932).

in his efforts (which proved fruitless) to secure regular Soviet contributions to *Pacific Affairs*.[42]

In 1939 Carter, who apparently did not realize that Moscow was soon to end all active cooperation with the IPR, wrote Lattimore suggesting that he placate the Soviets by giving collective security full treatment in *Pacific Affairs*. Lattimore replied that he was willing to do this, but noted previous criticism alleging that the IPR was either anti-Japanese or anti-British. However, he thought that rebuttals to an upcoming article critical of collective security might furnish a good start for a slow development of new support for this doctrine.[43] Reality, however, did not match the hope. No strong current for collective security developed from the pages of *Pacific Affairs*.

Serious questions about the objectivity of Lattimore's editorship did not end with the failure to establish a "general line" in *Pacific Affairs*. Of equal importance was his selection of authors and editing of individual contributions. In evaluating these factors, it is necessary to give some appreciation to the nature of the times. For most Americans the 1930's were characterized by economic depression at home and the growth of fascist states abroad. The impact on the American intellectual community was strong. To many, the survival of American capitalism seemed in doubt and socialism of various forms an attractive alternative; especially in cities such as New York, a large, amorphous leftist sector of opinion sprang into existence. Marxists and non-Marxists contributed to the same journals and few editors inquired about an author's political beliefs. Non-Communists sometimes cooperated with Communists in various causes in the belief that all were seeking similar goals.[44]

In such an atmosphere it would have been unusual had not some of the contributors to *Pacific Affairs* been Marxists or at least influenced by elements of Marxian thought. There is no evidence from Lattimore's writings that he personally

42. "Meeting on Pacific Affairs," undated memorandum, Vancouver Files. Lattimore to V.E. Motylev, June 2, 1937, *McCarran Hearings*, p. 3241.

43. Lattimore to Carter, August 9, 1939, Vancouver Files.

44. See Arthur M. Schlesinger, Jr., *The Politics of Upheaval* (Cambridge, Mass.: Riverside Press, 1960), pp. 160-68, 197-201.

accepted a Marxist view of the Asian scene. If anything, his writings show a lack of sophistication about Marxist theory and Soviet policy. What did intrigue Lattimore, however, was generalization and synthesis. In the 1930's, a number of writers offering such analyses were Marxists. The major question was how Lattimore would react to their contributions.

In a few cases, Lattimore ran Marxist analyses in *Pacific Affairs* with a clear indication of their viewpoint.[45] But a different response by Lattimore to Marxist contributions is indicated by his handling of a draft article by William Brandt for the September 1940 issue of *Pacific Affairs*. Field had apparently seen a copy and wrote Lattimore to the effect that the article would provide a very tough job of editing. He continued: "I also have the impression that, while the analysis is a straight Marxist one and from that point of view should not be altered, there are a great many of those over used Communist words and phrases which will make most of your readers vomit and which can very easily be paraphrased to the great benefit of the article. I am under the impression that this is a really very brilliant piece of work."[46]

Lattimore did not accept Field's description of the article as "Marxist." However, he thought that Brandt's piece would be a "good stout core around which to build the whole of the September [1940] issue of *Pacific Affairs*."[47] After what seems to have been extensive editing, the article appeared, sans Marxist verbiage, as an ambitious attempt to correlate the economic policies of the big powers with prospects for economic development in China.[48]

Several other examples suggest that Lattimore, while lacking a detailed understanding of Marxist theory or of the precise political position of his contributors, attempted to minimize open expressions of Marxian analysis in IPR publications. In 1935 he suggested to Field that an article by Hansu Chan (a pseudonym for International IPR staff mem-

45. See, for example, Isaacs, "Perspectives of the Chinese Revolution."
46. *McCarran Hearings*, p. 3249.
47. Ibid., p. 3250.
48. See William Brandt, "The United States, China, and the World Market," *Pacific Affairs*, 13 (September 1940): 279-319.

ber Chi Ch'ao-ting) be edited by Field in such a way that the American IPR could not be accused of approving a Stalinist view of events in China.[49] Four years later, he told James S. Allen, an infrequent contributor of articles on the Philippines, that he would look forward to future contributions but not right away, since the Philippine IPR might gain the impression that *Pacific Affairs* was printing only "radical stuff" about the Philippines.[50]

On another occasion Lattimore sent Field an article by "Asiaticus," the pen name of Hans Mueller, a left-wing German author residing in China. Lattimore explained that it would read too much like propaganda for inclusion in *Pacific Affairs*, but he hoped that Field could place it somewhere else.[51] Lattimore did, however, carry several other articles by Asiaticus. All but one provide few clues to the author's political position. That article, however, contains unmistakable traces of Marxist analysis. In the March 1938 issue of *Pacific Affairs*, Asiaticus argued that the 1927 Nationalist purge of Communist elements in Shanghai had been a "ruthless struggle against the democratic-revolutionary activities of the people's masses."[52]

An examination of the issues of *Pacific Affairs* under Lattimore's editorship reveals a desire to tone down, not highlight, contributions from Marxist authors. The major question seems not whether Lattimore presented Marxist analysis, but whether he was honest with his readers in failing to illustrate the political position of some of his contributors. By removing vocabulary which suggested a Marxist viewpoint, Lattimore left the impression with some readers that authors such as Asiaticus were objective observers making every effort to secure the closest possible approximation to reality. Many today might regard that impression as false.

Lattimore himself was concerned over the frictions which developed in the IPR over the Sino-Japanese War. The basic

49. Lattimore to Field, September 27, 1935, Vancouver Files.
50. Lattimore to James S. Allen, February 27, 1939, Vancouver Files.
51. Lattimore to Field, October 17, 1940, Vancouver Files.
52. See Asiaticus, "China's Advance From Defeat to Strength," *Pacific Affairs*, 11 (March 1938): 23.

problem, he believed, was that those who wanted to avoid controversy submitted advice but not articles. Thus, there had been a decrease in "temperate" contributions and an increase in "outspoken" ones.[53] It was a problem for which he could find no answer.

As full-scale Sino-Japanese war became a reality in 1937 in the wake of Japan's unprovoked attack at the Marco Polo Bridge near Peking, Americans generally and writers in particular expressed increasing sympathy with China's plight as a victim of Japanese aggression. Thus, it was no surprise that coverage of the war by *Pacific Affairs* on the whole favored the Chinese side. Such sympathy did not go unnoticed, however. In the December 1938 issue Lattimore informed his readers about a letter from a member of the Canadian IPR, criticizing *Pacific Affairs* for one-sided presentation of the Sino-Japanese conflict. Lattimore defended his own approach to the problem but suggested that readers write in and let him know their views.[54] A few did, but there was no consensus on how to solve the problem.

Although it was not widely recognized at the time, an even more difficult question for *Pacific Affairs* was its treatment of the budding Chinese Communist movement. A number of factors combined to limit both the extent and quality of IPR analysis of the CCP during Lattimore's editorship (1933-41). Relatively few writers gained access to the Communist areas of China, and few of those had sufficient training in Communist doctrine or practice to offer knowledgeable estimates of CCP activities. In addition, few people at that time had any idea that the Communists were a force which might eventually control all of China.

The result was that IPR readers were provided only with infrequent and shallow coverage of the Chinese Communist movement. For example, the September 1938 issue of *Pacific Affairs* carried an interview with a CCP official by Nym Wales. On closer inspection, however, the "interview" turned out to be only one open-ended question followed by a long statement from the Communist official, Politburo member

53. Owen Lattimore, "Report of the Editor of Pacific Affairs," December 22, 1938, Vancouver Files.

54. *Pacific Affairs*, 11 (December 1938): 495-96.

Lo Fu (Chang Wen-t'ien).[55] No effort was apparently made by the author to raise follow-up questions or to provide the reader with some background on the significance of the statements. Another frequent defect—the uncritical use of CCP sources—was illustrated by Anna Louise Strong's June 1941 article on Communist guerrilla units.[56] But no articles under Lattimore's editorship left the reader with the impression that the CCP was anything but a genuine Communist movement.

After Lattimore's resignation as editor in 1941, *Pacific Affairs* gradually began to lose some of its previous flamboyance and air of controversy. It continued to handle political questions, but without much flair.

Far Eastern Survey

A very different course was followed by *Far Eastern Survey*, the journal of the American Council. That it did so was testimony to the variety which existed in the IPR, as well as evidence of the complex personality of Frederick Vanderbilt Field.

While Owen Lattimore was seeking to make *Pacific Affairs* more lively and controversial, just the opposite path was chosen by Russell Shiman, first editor of the *Survey*. Shiman believed that his journal should stick mainly to fundamental economic matters in the tradition of early IPR research. As a result, *Far Eastern Survey* prior to 1941 was generally a dry collection of articles on economic conditions in Asia. Its occasional forays into the political realm were invariably factually oriented and sparked none of the controversies surrounding its sister publication.

Not all IPR staff members were happy with this situation. In 1938 International IPR staffers Ch'en Han-seng and Elsie Fairfax-Chomeley wrote Edward Carter to complain about the *Survey's* economic orientation. Both thought it should become more controversial and less "balanced" and

55. Nym Wales, "Why the Chinese Communists Support the United Front: An Interview with Lo Fu," *Pacific Affairs*, 11 (September 1938): 311-22.

56. Anna Louise Strong, "Eighth Route Regions in North China," *Pacific Affairs*, 14 (June 1941): 154-65.

that the individual writer should take responsibility for his own article.[57]

As secretary of the American Council, Frederick Field was in a key position to influence the course of *Far Eastern Survey*. The evidence suggests that Field first approved of Shiman's policies; later he proposed a change but was unwilling to institute it when opposition developed.

During his first four years as secretary (1934-38), Field apparently agreed with the *Survey*'s economic emphasis. At that time he stated the view that IPR publications should concentrate on fundamental research rather than "hot" political subjects.[58] As the Sino-Japanese conflict broadened, Field began to edge away from his earlier position. In 1937 he helped to establish the journal *Amerasia* as a focus for criticism of Japanese actions. As he later explained it, he considered *Amerasia* a vehicle by which IPR writers could express views considered inappropriate for IPR publications.[59]

By 1939, however, Field apparently had come to the conclusion that the *Survey* should give comprehensive treatment to Far Eastern political problems. He therefore proposed that the American Council take over *Amerasia* and utilize it to present all sides of Asian political questions.

In presenting his proposal to the Board of Trustees, Field undoubtedly foresaw at least two possible grounds of criticism. The most obvious was that the American Council would risk the sort of controversy already generated by *Pacific Affairs*. The other was that *Amerasia*, rightly or wrongly, was regarded with suspicion in some American academic circles. Field had discussed the problem a year earlier in a facetiously worded letter to Edward Carter:

I am also interested to know that Payson Treat of Stanford has a private file showing the past history of the editors of *Amerasia* and is spreading the story that it is a united front and therefore a Bolshevik supported magazine. I would bet twenty to one that his history of the editors is inaccurate for very few of us know all the underground and nefarious activities which they have for years been carrying on. The whole board, of course, would be deported from the

57. "Private Memorandum for Mr. Carter from Ch'en Han-seng and Elsie," October 21, 1937, Columbia Files.
58. Lattimore to Catherine Porter, March 31, 1938, Columbia Files.
59. *McCarran Hearings*, p. 115.

country immediately if any of this information came to light. It would also be impossible without having photostats of our accounts to know precisely how much money was coming in from Moscow each month.[60]

Field circulated his proposal to the Board of Trustees and asked for comments. A majority favored the idea, including Carter who thought that *Amerasia*'s editorial policy was more in line with what American IPR members wanted than that of *Far Eastern Survey*.[61] However, several important trustees, notably Carl Alsberg and Philip Jessup, opposed the idea. Field apparently decided not to go ahead with his proposal. Despite his own feelings, he did not press the matter during the remainder of his term as secretary.

Only after Field and Russell Shiman had left their positions was Carter successful in implementing a shift in the *Far Eastern Survey*. In 1941 the *Survey* began gingerly to expand its coverage of political subjects. Relatively little controversy was encountered until July 1943 with the publication of an article by T. A. Bisson on the Chinese political situation. Bisson argued that there were really two Chinas, "democratic" (Communist) China and "feudal" (Nationalist) China. In what was probably the first—but not the last—claim in the *Survey* that the CCP was practicing agrarian radicalism rather than communism, Bisson claimed that the local guerrilla structure was more akin to an agrarian "bourgeois democracy" than to communism. Because the Nationalist areas were based on the "landlord-usurer system," he maintained they could properly be called "feudal."[62]

As might have been expected, Chinese Nationalist reaction was vigorous. C. L. Hsia, head of the Chinese News Service in New York, sent in a biting protest defending the National Government and criticizing Bisson's use of the term *feudal*. Hsia attempted without success to get both the American and Pacific councils to disown the article. A reply from the editors emphasized that Bisson's position was his own and

60. Field to Carter, September 6, 1938, Columbia Files.
61. Carter to Field, August 27, 1939, Columbia Files.
62. T. A. Bisson, "China's Part in a Coalition War," *Far Eastern Survey*, 12 (July 14, 1943): 135-41.

not that of the American Council.[63] However, the controversy was enough to dull at least temporarily the enthusiasm of the editors for similar articles.[64]

Other Publications

While journals such as *Pacific Affairs* and *Far Eastern Survey* secured more popular interest, a good portion of the IPR's real product in Far Eastern research was contained in other publications. Especially important was IPR support for book publishing on Asian topics. Relatively few of these works, whether by IPR staffers or other authors, stirred great controversy; many made significant contributions to their fields.

One set of volumes did involve significant policy issues, however—the Inquiry Series. Conceived by the International Secretariat as an effort to investigate the Sino-Japanese conflict, the project posed very serious questions about the continued viability of the Japanese Council within the IPR. For many years the Japanese had argued, often unsuccessfully, against treatment of Sino-Japanese differences in IPR publications. IPR sponsorship of a multivolume inquiry into the subject would likely place officials of the Japanese IPR in a delicate situation.

The Japanese argued that the Inquiry would involve the IPR in too political a field. In addition, they thought that staff members of the International Secretariat were not the proper people to undertake this type of research.[65] In spite of these objections, the project was begun in 1938. The Japanese Council declared it could not participate and dissociated itself in advance with the results.[66]

Perhaps in part because of Japanese objections, three advisers were named to review contributions to the Inquiry. The final volumes were of uneven quality. Some, such as *Economic Shanghai* by Robert Barnett and George Taylor's

63. C. L. Hsia to Carter, August 3, 1943, Columbia Files. The editor's note is in *Far Eastern Survey*, 12 (August 11, 1943): 157.

64. William L. Holland, personal interview, March 27, 1970.

65. "Private Memorandum from ECC to the Files Regarding the Visit of Dr. Takayangi," undated, Columbia Files.

66. IPR, *Problems of the Pacific, 1939* (New York, 1940), p. v.

The Struggle for North China, were well received. Others such as William Mandel's *The Soviet Far East and Central Asia* and Harriet Moore's *Soviet Far Eastern Policy*, were notable for their lack of incisive analysis about Soviet aims and their uncritical use of Soviet materials. Moore's work was published despite the fact that one adviser refused twice to pass it, terming it "propaganda."[67]

Although no one realized it at the time, the Inquiry produced an exchange of correspondence which would return to haunt the IPR. As was his penchant, Edward Carter sent Owen Lattimore a copy of a letter about the Inquiry and requested his comments. Part of Lattimore's response, which later came to be termed the "cagey letter," follows:

. . . I think that you are pretty cagey in turning over so much of the China section of the inquiry to Asiaticus, Han-seng, and Chi. They will bring out the absolutely essential radical aspects, but can be depended on to do it with the right touch.

For the general purposes of this inquiry it seems to me that the good scoring position, for the IPR, differs with different countries. For China, my hunch is that it will pay to keep behind the official Chinese Communist position—far enough not to be covered by the same label—but enough ahead of the active Chinese liberals to be noticeable. . . . For the U.S.S.R.—back their international policy in general, but without using their slogans and above all without giving them or anybody else an impression of subservience. . . .[68]

Lattimore, of course, had no responsibility for the Inquiry and his suggestions were not implemented.[69] Refusal to accept his advice was not unusual, since many staff members regarded him as brilliant and witty, but often imprecise or wrong.[70] They were willing to overlook or ignore the latter qualities in order to appreciate the former. In later times, others were not so generous.

THE IPR AND OUTSIDE ACTIVITIES

As Sino-Japanese hostilities increased during 1937 and 1938, many Asian specialists felt compelled to speak out against Japanese aggression. Some joined a budding series of commit-

67. Condliffe to Benjamin Mandel, September 18, 1951, Condliffe Papers.

68. Lattimore to Carter, July 10, 1938, in *McCarran Hearings*, p. 40.

69. Carter to Lattimore, July 19, 1938, Vancouver Files.

70. Dorothy Borg, personal interview, May 9, 1963.

tees designed either to assist the Chinese or to deny Japan any use of United States goods. Thus the IPR and its various national councils were faced with a difficult question: should they advise their staff members to avoid activities which might increase frictions within the organization? As in the case of IPR publications, the answer was neither predictable nor consistent.

At the American Council there was a rule against staff participation in organizations aiding either belligerent. Frederick Field cited the prohibition in rejecting an invitation to join the China Emergency Civilian Relief as well as the American Committee for Chinese Industrial Cooperatives.[71]

Of course, the American Council's rule did not prohibit many actions which might have caused friction with the Japanese Council or with Americans who were concerned with too public an identification of IPR officials with political action groups. Despite his own leftward political metamorphosis, Frederick Field seems to have appreciated these problems.

Field's political sophistication was evident in 1939 in a reply to Carter concerning an "Open Letter to Active Sponsors of Democracy and Peace." Field said that he was sympathetic but would not sign it. "It is from these lists that outfits like the Dies Committee get their names, and I should very much prefer in the next few years going about my work without unnecessarily throwing my name around."[72] Perhaps with similar foresight, he told an official of the American League against War and Fascism that he wanted any connection between himself and the league kept confidential.[73] Field also adopted a cautious attitude on public writings. He was willing to help establish and contribute to *Amerasia*, but apparently thought it best to use a pen name for an article in the strongly leftist *China Today*.

Field's sense of caution about involving the IPR in outside activities was uncharacteristically missing on one occasion. In 1938 he recommended that the American Council become

71. Field to Colonel Theodore Roosevelt, December 23, 1937, Columbia Files.
72. Field to Carter, July 24, 1939, Columbia Files.
73. Field to Paul M. Reid, April 21, 1936, Columbia Files.

affiliated "in a consultative capacity" with the National
Peace Conference. The Board of Trustees turned him down—
unanimously.[74]

Caution was never a notable attribute of Edward Carter.
Impulsive and energetic, Carter occasionally displayed in his
outside activities the same type of promotional instincts which
had secured him leadership in the IPR. An example is contained in his 1938 reply to a proposal by Philip Jaffe that the
United States initiate a reconstruction loan to China following the end of Sino-Japanese hostilities. Carter thought it a
good idea and replied that when it was in final form, the two
of them should try to sell it privately to President Roosevelt,
Cordell Hull, Henry Wallace, Communist party chief Earl
Browder, and others.[75]

Carter's desire for improved Soviet-United States relations
as well as his personal penchant for hobnobbing with official-
dom often resulted in social contacts with Soviet officials.
These contacts continued long after the Soviet Council had
ceased to show any active interest in the IPR. He also took a
leading role in the American-Russian Institute, despite his
concern that very few on its board were not "associated in
the public mind with a strongly pro-Russian bias."[76]

One incident in 1942 stands out as evidence of Carter's lack
of good judgment in his outside activities. In that year he wrote
the War Department to suggest that Frederick Field be
considered for a position in United States military intelligence.
The suggestion was rebuffed.[77]

Owen Lattimore was not by nature a joiner. He did join the
editorial board of *Amerasia*, but mentioned his IPR connection in refusing a similar position at *China Today*, which he
described as "more obviously partisan" than *Amerasia*[78]—
Lattimore took a very serious view about the course of Far
Eastern developments, however, and felt a strong need to
express his views in public lectures.

Edward Carter at first was not inclined to suggest restraint

74. Field to Arthur D. Reeve, Jr. January 5, 1940, Columbia Files.
75. Carter to Philip Jaffe, May 12, 1938, Vancouver Files.
76. Carter to Harriet Moore, June 7, 1943, Columbia Files.
77. *McCarran Hearings*, p. 11.
78. Lattimore to Max Granich, December 13, 1939, Vancouver Files.

on the part of the man he had selected to edit *Pacific Affairs*. He no doubt realized that it would be difficult to restrain Lattimore's public statements in view of the latter's position as only a part-time editor who also held his own professorial appointment. Carter's reluctance to counsel his colleague was likely bolstered by the realization that freedom of expression and absence of rigid staff rules were probably among the key factors which made work with the IPR most satisfying. But Carter's concern about the effect of Lattimore's speech-making and writing on IPR unity apparently increased during the first part of 1938. In part, his concern may have been stimulated by criticism of Lattimore by IPR founder Frank Atherton. Atherton wrote to say he thought that Lattimore had been too behemently anti-Japanese during a speech in Hawaii.[79] Criticism from the Japanese Council was likely another factor.

Replying to Lattimore's "cagey" letter and its suggestions about the proper "scoring position" for the Inquiry, Carter delivered what amounted to a mildly phrased rebuke. He noted that members of the Secretariat staff were "servants of all eleven Councils" and concluded, "If in our private capacities we take a line that is so conspicuous that a large element in our constituency feels that we cannot administer our international responsibilities with impartiality then I think that our non-Secretariat activities should be reconsidered." Carter mentioned that he had ceased writing for *Amerasia* and suggested that Lattimore resign his position on the *Amerasia* editorial board.[80]

Despite continued pressure from Carter during the next month, Lattimore held firm to the view that he was primarily an independent observer and commentator who should be free to express his own views.[81] He maintained that these views were well known and therefore it would look "silly" and "timid" for him now to avoid further expression of such attitudes.[82]

In face of Lattimore's determined position, Carter retreated.

79. Atherton to Lattimore, February 10, 1938, Columbia Files.
80. Carter to Lattimore, July 19, 1938, Columbia Files.
81. Lattimore to William L. Holland, May 5, 1952, Columbia Files.
82. Lattimore to Carter, July 10, 1938, Vancouver Files.

In the final analysis he was unwilling to discipline his colleague and friend. Having failed to restrain Lattimore, of course,
he was in a poor position to restrict the activities of other
staff members. When a prominent member of the Hawaii IPR
sent a stiff protest about participation of IPR personnel in
the American Committee for Non-Participation in Japanese
Aggression, he could reply only that he had held his own
attitude in check.[83]

Thus, by 1939 the IPR had largely failed to establish clear
rules restricting its employees from engaging in outside
activities which might raise questions about the Institute's
neutrality in the Sino-Japanese conflict. The failure to set up
rigid rules was no doubt favored by the staff, many of whom
had joined the IPR precisely because of its relatively unfet-
tered climate for creativity. By the same token, however, the
IPR's inaction exacerbated the already difficult position of
the Japanese Council and brought forth criticism from some
influential members of the American Council.

REGIONALISM IN THE AMERICAN COUNCIL

Both geography and financial power assured the American
Council a predominant position within the IPR. Far more
than with any other council, the fortunes of the International
IPR were interlocked with those of the American Council.
Americans and American foundations always provided the
bulk of IPR contributions. American personnel were key to
the success of the International Secretariat, despite the
attempt of Edward Carter to internationalize his staff.

New York provided both the physical headquarters and
financial center for the American Council. The secretary of
the American Council was normally based there together with
a small staff, located in the same offices occupied by the
International Secretariat. Meetings of the decision-making
Board of Trustees and its Executive Committee were commonly held there.

But many members of the American Council resided far
from New York, and herein lay the crux of one of its most
difficult problems: regionalism. Several local chapters were

83. Wallace M. Alexander to Carter, January 20, 1939, Columbia
Files; Carter to Alexander, undated, Columbia Files.

formed, the most powerful of which were in Hawaii, San
Francisco, and Seattle. These chapters contained a number of
people influential in the early years of the IPR, some of whom
were uneasy about the shift of the International IPR to New
York and the rise of Edward Carter to leadership within the
organization. On the whole, the leaders of these chapters
tended to support the more restrictive vision favored by early
IPR leaders; they were often more concerned than some in
New York about outside activities of institute officials which
might subject them and their chapters to criticism in their
communities. Often they were jealous of the prerogatives of
the New York office and desirous of greater autonomy for their
own groups.

A good insight into regionalism in the American Council
can be obtained from a brief look at the San Francisco Bay
Region Chapter. Organized in the late twenties, the San
Francisco Chapter was often at odds with IPR headquarters
in New York. In part, the differences were those one might
normally expect to find between East Coast and West Coast.
San Franciscans usually chafe at the notion that they should
take a back seat to New Yorkers. Some San Francisco members
also believed their city a more logical place for American IPR
headquarters than New York.

Personal and practical issues were also involved. Friction
developed between Edward Carter and several San Francisco
IPR leaders, because of a feeling that Carter had taken actions without adequate consultation with leaders in San
Francisco. In addition, some Bay Region leaders were concerned over certain of Carter's outside activities which they
thought might reflect unfavorably on the San Francisco
group.[84] Division of membership dues was also in dispute;
Bay Region officials naturally wanted to retain a good portion of the dues for activities in San Francisco. The New
York office, often hard pressed for funds, also wanted an important share.

During his tenure as secretary of the American Council
(1934-40), Frederick Field attempted to deal with questions
of regionalism. In late 1937 he went to San Francisco and for
several months administered the American group from the

84. John B. Condliffe, personal interview, April 14, 1970.

West Coast. Personal relations between Field and San Francisco leaders seemed good, although the visit raised unwarranted hopes that American IPR headquarters might be transferred permanently to the Bay Area.[85]

Not long after Field returned to New York, however, the honeymoon was over. This time the issue was financial cooperation. In January 1940 a letter from the officers of the American Council accused the San Francisco Chapter of unilaterally altering agreements on retention of dues. The letter cited the "ultimate authority of the National Council" in such matters.[86] The secretary of the Bay Region group disagreed, saying that San Francisco considered itself an "autonomous regional group."[87] A compromise was eventually worked out, but friction remained between San Francisco and the head office.

Field was unable to make any notable progress on several issues which he perceptively felt needed attention. The first was the relationship between the American and Pacific councils. Field proposed that ultimately a "sharp distinction" should be drawn between the two councils and that both should have separate offices and staffs.[88] The idea was a good one, but financial considerations made it unfeasible.

The failure of the Board of Trustees to give adequate direction to the American Council also bothered Field. In 1936 he wrote one trustee to complain that neither the board nor its Executive Committee really existed off paper. "Because," he wrote, "of the geographical distribution of the officers it is naturally impossible for them to supervise our activities as carefully as continuously as I should like to have some responsible body of the organization do."[89] Field hoped to remedy the situation in part by suggesting creation of a

85. San Francisco IPR, Minutes of Executive Committee Meeting, September 21, 1937, from the Papers of Mrs. Alfred McLaughlin, Bancroft Library, University of California, Berkeley (hereafter cited as McLaughlin Papers).

86. Philip Jessup to Ray Lyman Wilbur, January 31, 1940, McLaughlin Papers.

87. John H. Oakie to Ray Lyman Wilbur, February 6, 1940, McLaughlin Papers.

88. Field to Carter, October 12, 1938, Columbia Files.

89. Field to Joseph Chamberlin, October 23, 1936, Columbia Files.

smaller, more responsible and active Executive Committee, but this was not realized.[90]

On one issue, Field was able to make a direct contribution: money. The American Council was constantly in perilous financial health and in need of emergency financial injections. Between 1929 and 1948, Field provided more than fifty thousand dollars of his own funds to support the IPR.[91] Often his contributions came at key times which allowed the institute to avoid crippling retrenchments.

By 1940 Field was highly regarded as an able and affable secretary. His leftward political metamorphosis had been quiet, without obvious landmarks, and therefore did not rouse the concern of the trustees or members of the IPR. By the summer of that year, however, Field had decided upon a step which he knew would tarnish his image in the IPR: he would accept a position with the American Peace Mobilization. An ostensibly pacifist group protesting possible American involvement in the European war, the APM later exhibited convincing signs of subservience to the policies of the American Communists.

Field quickly decided that his only course was to resign his position as secretary of the American Council. He discussed the matter with Trustee Philip Jessup, who urged him to stay. Field replied that his mission might be misinterpreted and that he should terminate all connection with the IPR.[92] In explaining his position to the Executive Committee, Field asserted that in view of possible criticism and his concern for the welfare of the IPR, he would have to resign from all institute responsibilities.[93]

The Board of Trustees accepted Field's resignation as secretary with the statement that he would be "eagerly welcomed back" to the IPR staff when he had completed his new undertaking.[94] Curiously, however, Field did not resign

90. Field to Catherine Porter, October 4, 1934, Columbia Files.
91. Katrine Greene to Clayton Lane, March 2, 1949, Columbia Files.
92. Edward C. Carter, Memorandum, October 29, 1940, Columbia Files.
93. American Council, IPR, Minutes of Executive Committee Meeting, September 18, 1940, Columbia Files.
94. American Council, IPR, Minutes of Board of Trustees Meeting,

his position on the board, despite his earlier inclination to sever all connections with the institute. In his report to the board, Field stressed his desire to return to research as a primary cause of his departure—the explanation passed out to local IPR chapters.[95] Thus, most IPR members were unaware of Field's true reasons for resigning or the possible problems of his continued presence on the board.

THE IPR IN WARTIME

During the better part of two decades, the IPR had prided itself as a private organization free from government control or influence. Although several of the national councils, notably those from France and the Soviet Union, did not meet such qualifications, the International IPR and the American Council were clearly under private control. As late as 1938, Frederick Field had vetoed a suggestion that the American Council set up an office in Washington, D.C., on the grounds that it might lead to lobbying activities by IPR personnel.[96]

America's sudden entry into World War II left the IPR little choice about forging stronger links to government. Washington's need for Asian specialists and background material on the Far East was immense; the IPR quickly rose to the challenge. Many IPR staff members joined the government; never before had IPR publications been in such demand. In 1942 the American Council reversed itself and established a Washington office to facilitate cooperation in the war effort.[97]

By 1944 the future of the Institute of Pacific Relations appeared bright. True, it had failed badly in its objective of improving the relations among Pacific nations. However, the institute had survived some difficult times and taken some basic decisions which had brought it pre-eminent status among Asian studies groups in the United States and abroad.

November 25, 1940, Columbia Files.

95. Frederick V. Field, "Report of the Secretary to the Board of Trustees," June 28, 1940, Columbia Files.

96. Field to Catherine Porter, January 27, 1938, Columbia Files.

97. American Council, IPR, *The IPR in Wartime* (New York, 1941), p. 10.

To be sure, some basic problems remained. Neither the Pacific Council nor the trustees of the American Council had provided adequate leadership to the staff. Some influential members of the American Council were uneasy about the IPR's course and others were disturbed by what seemed like personal indiscretions of some institute leaders. But few in 1944 doubted that the IPR would enter the postwar period in strong condition.

It was in this atmosphere that the IPR received its first major attack.

2

Kohlberg and the "China Lobby": The Charges Alter (1944-49)

As has been noted, criticism of the IPR during its first twenty years was largely internal. For the most part, it was based on differing notions of the nature of the organization or disagreements about possible conflicts of interest between an official's IPR role and his outside activities. Essentially, these could be described as academic criticisms from persons who were directly concerned with the IPR's welfare. Occasionally, a critic would accuse the institute of pro-Chinese or even pro-Japanese sympathies. Few of these charges were given great notice, however, and none resulted in serious harm to the IPR.

By late 1943, however, a slow change began to appear in criticism directed at the IPR. This time the charge was pro-communism and the accusers were more often interested in China policy than the IPR *per se*. The timing of these new and ultimately damaging charges was not accidental. It coincided with a growing concern on the part of a small number of Chinese Nationalist supporters in America about the fate of the Chinese National government. They had waited for several frustrating years while the United States ignored their pleas for heavy military aid to President Chiang Kai-shek. Now they were concerned by reports that the war was not going well for China: they reacted with indignation to what they considered a growing campaign by American newsmen and writers to "smear" the reputation of the National government with reports of extensive corruption and inefficiency. They fought back by seeking to discredit their foes in the press and academia. Since many of these writers and newsmen were members of the IPR, it was only a matter of time before the institute itself came under attack.

An examination of the early issues of the *China Monthly* illustrates this process. Begun in 1939 as a Catholic-oriented journal to support China in the Sino-Japanese War, it first discouraged United States involvement in the European conflict and called for a trade embargo against Japan. After Pearl Harbor and America's declaration of war on the Axis powers, the *China Monthly* urged Washington to give priority to the Pacific front and especially China. Failing in this effort and seeing signs of danger for the beleaguered Chinese government, the *China Monthly* began to question the motives of those who favored a different policy. By February 1943 it began to talk vaguely about unnamed "Red Second-fronters" who were willing to lavish aid on Russia but not on China.[1] By September it issued its first attack on the IPR in the form of a slashing critique of T. A. Bisson's July 1943 article for the *Far Eastern Survey* delineating a "democratic" and "feudal" China. A *China Monthly* editorial termed him "Comrade Bisson" and said his position was "openly pro-Communist."[2]

Given the context of events in the Far East and the eventual development of the Cold War, it seems likely that the IPR would have been subjected to occasional charges of "procommunism." However, the extent of these charges and to some degree their effectiveness in damaging the IPR's public image were largely the work of one man—Alfred Kohlberg.

Before 1944 neither the public nor the IPR had heard much of Kohlberg. An obscure businessman, he had gone to China in 1916 and, like many others, had developed an immediate liking for the Chinese people. During the next few decades he organized an extensive business in imported Chinese embroideries. Although his offices were in America, Kohlberg made frequent trips to China to oversee the manufacture of his products and to renew friendships with Chinese acquaintances. Along with many other businessmen, he joined the

1. *China Monthly*, 3 (February 1943): 3.
2. Ibid., 4 (September 1943): 5.

IPR but took no active part at first, giving its publications little attention.

World War II shook Kohlberg's complacence about Far Eastern affairs and propelled him into sharp conflict with the IPR. At first, he accepted Japan's explanation for its occupation of Manchuria. In 1939 he entered Japanese-occupied South China and, despite a leg wound suffered when his craft was fired upon by a Japanese gunboat in the Han River, managed to arrange an agreement with the Japanese by which products destined for America could be shipped out of Swatow.[3]

By 1940, however, Kohlberg had decided that Japan was actually planning the conquest of China.[4] Normally a rather gentle and mild-spoken individual, he reacted strongly to this realization. So strong was his concern that in July 1940 he offered himself as a kamikaze pilot to the Royal Canadian Air Force. He repeated the offer the next year to an assistant secretary of the United States Navy.[5] His sense of outrage about Japanese aggression was also transferred to the IPR. As Kohlberg explained it later, he felt that "gangster" powers were at work in the Far East and that therefore he could not "support any organization attempting an unprejudiced study of the rights and wrongs of the situation. The need at the moment is to catch, prosecute and punish the gangsters, . . ."[6] In 1940 he resigned from the IPR, but later withdrew the resignation at the urging of Edward Carter.[7] Nevertheless, the incident was a sign of the passion and single-mindedness which this normally placid individual could occasionally summon against those with whom he did not agree.

1943 was clearly a turning point for Kohlberg and, ultimate-

3. Alfred Kohlberg, "To My Grandchildren," p. 63. I am indebted to Professor Lawrence Kohlberg for the opportunity of reviewing this unpublished autobiography.

4. Ibid.

5. Ibid., p. 82b.

6. Alfred Kohlberg, 88-page document on the IPR (mimeographed), p. 10, as cited in Donald Oberdorfer, Jr., "The McCarran Committee's Investigation of the Institute of Pacific Relations" (senior thesis, Princeton University, 1952), p. 9. I wish to thank Mr. Oberdorfer for the opportunity of reviewing this work.

7. Oberdorfer, "The McCarran Committee's Investigation," p. 8.

ly, the IPR. As a director of the American Bureau for Medical Aid to China (ABMAC), a member of United China Relief, Kohlberg was asked to utilize one of his periodic trips to China to check the efficiency and effectiveness of ABMAC's program. Before leaving for the Far East, Kohlberg talked with Lauchlin Currie, an assistant to President Roosevelt. Currie told him of reports of graft in aid to China.[8]

Currie's report was perplexing, and Kohlberg was determined to check it out carefully. Upon arriving in Chungking, he received confirmation of such charges from Americans involved in aid to China. Kohlberg was not satisfied and resolved to go into the field and verify the allegations. Over the strong opposition of both the ABMAC and United China Relief directors in Chungking and without obtaining the required permit from the Chinese government, Kohlberg went into the field to check for himself. After questioning Chinese friends at the medical headquarters at Kweiyang, he decided that the stories of graft were inaccurate or exaggerated. He checked several other facilities with the same results.[9] Upon returning to Chungking, Kohlberg sought out Edward Carter, who was visiting China on behalf of United China Relief. He was unable to obtain Carter's cooperation in registering a complaint against Dwight Edwards, United China Relief director in Chungking.[10]

After his return to the United States, Kohlberg attempted to get ABMAC to recall the "liars" who were spreading stories of corruption. His charges were not upheld, however, and ABMAC turned down his resolution to withdraw from United China Relief. Kohlberg then resigned from ABMAC.[11]

By early 1944 Kohlberg was a confused man. By his own thinking the Chinese government was being vilified with unfair charges of corruption; he had pointed this out to the responsible authorities but received no redress. How could such conduct be explained? He related his concern to Dr.

8. Kohlberg, "To My Grandchildren," p. 84.

9. Kohlberg, "To My Grandchildren," pp. 85-86.

10. Joseph Keeley, *The China Lobby Man* (New Rochelle, N.Y.: Arlington House, 1969), p. 67.

11. Kohlberg, "To My Grandchildren," p. 88.

Maurice William, a New York dentist and ex-Socialist. William's answer was to become Kohlberg's credo: it was the Communists acting through the IPR.[12]

Characteristically, Kohlberg did not immediately accept Dr. William's accusation against the IPR, but decided to investigate the matter himself. He launched a six-month research project at the New York Public Library to compare IPR publications for 1937-44 with Communist publications for a similar period. Few other men would have had the time, money, or interest to engage in such a project. But Kohlberg was not like most other men. He had already made his money, his business was largely finished by the war, and it was time to conquer new fields.

Completing his research, Kohlberg found that it seemed to corroborate Dr. William's charge of Communist infiltration in in the IPR. Specifically, he determined that IPR publications had followed the Communist position on China in the following manner: (1) 1937-39, praise of Chiang Kai-Shek; (2) 1939-June 1941, criticism of Chiang; (3) June 22, 1941 (German invasion of Russia)-spring of 1943, praise; (4) spring of 1943-1944, criticism.[13]

A less impassioned observer, of course, might have recognized some fatal weaknesses in such an analysis. In the first place, Kohlberg had time only to review articles in *Pacific Affairs* and *Far Eastern Survey* plus a small number of other publications. He thus eliminated the bulk of IPR research contained in institute-supported books on China. Second, he had considered *Pacific Affairs* and *Far Eastern Survey* together, as if these publications were subject to central direction by a monolithic organization. As noted earlier, this was far from the case. In addition, Kohlberg apparently found it difficult to accept the fact that an author might both "praise" and "abuse" President Chiang or the National government in the same article. His mind simply did not work that way.

By late 1944 Kohlberg was ready to act. On November 9 he wrote Edward Carter outlining his major charges and suggesting that he conduct a housecleaning of unnamed Communists

12. Keeley, *The China Lobby Man*, pp. 75-76.
13. Kohlberg, "To My Grandchildren," p. 96.

in the IPR.[14] He attached a rambling, confusing eighty-eight-page document consisting largely of quotations from *Far Eastern Survey, Pacific Affairs,* and various Communist publications. To ensure a wide audience for his charges, Kohlberg sent copies to the IPR trustees and other influential members of the institute.

Probably none of the trustees was inclined to accept Kohlberg's charges, and few at the time thought such confused allegations would do much damage to the IPR. The American Council's Executive Committee met on November 11 and found "no reason to consider seriously the charge of bias."[15]

At this point and later, a less persistent man might have given up. But Kohlberg pushed on and made the IPR his full-time hobby for three vigorous years. He publicized his case with literally thousands of letters to IPR members and contributors, government officials, newspaper editors, and prominent citizens. Only a very few, such as the *Reader's Digest,* took Kohlberg's charges seriously at the time. A more typical reaction came from financier Thomas Lamont, whose private secretary told American Council Secretary Raymond Dennett that Lamont had "always realized that the charges were perfectly silly, . . ."[16]

Kohlberg was not deterred, however. Seeing that the IPR intended to take no action on his allegations, he demanded that his charges be investigated by a committee of persons having no connections with the IPR. The institute refused and offered instead an investigation by three persons of its own choosing. Kohlberg declined this suggestion and instituted court action to force the IPR to hand over its membership lists so that he could circulate IPR members and ask them to support his call for an investigation. After much delay, an agreement was finally reached to circulate the membership

14. Kohlberg to Carter, November 9, 1944, from the Files of the San Francisco IPR located in the archives section, Hoover Institution Library, Stanford University, Stanford, California (hereafter cited as Hoover Files).

15. IPR, circular letter to the Board of Trustees, December 19, 1944, Hoover Files.

16. Thomas W. Lamont to Raymond Dennett, undated, Columbia Files.

for proxies to be used in a general meeting in 1947 to decide
whether Kohlberg's investigation should go forward.[17]

In the meantime, Kohlberg began to fill in some details of
his accusation that Communists held positions within the IPR.
In retrospect, it seems unlikely that Kohlberg originally had
a very clear picture of which "Reds" he thought should be
fired. During 1945 and 1946, however, he came into contact
with a number of strong anti-Communists and ex-Communists
nists such as Isaac Don Levine and Louis Budenz. At that
point he began to formulate charges against specific IPR
officials or writers. In 1945, he asserted that IPR staff member
Y. Y. Hsu had been a Communist at Columbia and that he was
"either an officer or a paid employee of the New York Branch
of the Third International."[18] The next year he charged that
Abraham Chapman, an occasional contributor to *Pacific
Affairs*, was a member of the New York State Central
Committee of the Communist party.[19] By early 1947 he had
claimed that ten members of the Board of Trustees were "pro-
Communists."[20]

Kohlberg's easy use of the term, "pro-Communist," was a
fundamental feature of his campaign and a characteristic
which marked later charges against the IPR and United
States China policy. Kohlberg later explained what he meant
in an interview: "I mean by a pro-Communist a person whose
sympathies in the Far East were with the Communist forces.
I can't go into the mental processes. He might not be pro-
Communist in Europe. Philip Jessup, for instance, is probably
not a pro-Communist in Europe. I don't know whether he is
or not. But in the Far East he is pro-Communist."[21] By such a
device Kohlberg had not only transformed questions about the
IPR from the academic to the security field; he had also made
it unnecessary to produce concrete information corroborating
his charges that Communists had infiltrated the IPR staff.
The general charge of "procommunism" was just as effective
and, because of its vagueness, more difficult to counter.

17. Speech by Arthur Dean, April 22, 1947, Hoover Files.

18. Kohlberg to Galen Fisher, February 26, 1945, Columbia Files.

19. Kohlberg to Owen Lattimore, October 4, 1946, Columbia Files.

20. Charles Wertenbaker, "The World of Alfred Kohlberg," *Reporter*,
6 (April 29, 1952): 22.

21. Ibid., p. 20.

In addition to his extensive letter-writing campaign, Kohlberg publicized his charges against the IPR in numerous writings for the *China Monthly* and in *Plain Talk*, a journal which he established in 1946. Many of Kohlberg's articles did not deal specifically with the IPR, however, and their impact was probably confined to a fairly small circle of already sympathetic readers.

Although the American Council Executive Committee did not think Kohlberg's charges worthy of an extensive investigation, it nevertheless thought that some sort of reply should be provided for IPR members. The staff was directed to prepare a response and did so in the form of a fifty-two-page refutation of Kohlberg's charges. It asserted that Kohlberg had presented no evidence to support his charge of Communist activity by the staff "because none exists."[22] It went on to criticize Kohlberg's credentials to judge IPR publications as well as his selection of articles. In analyzing Kohlberg's four periods of "praise" and "abuse," the staff report found both praise and criticism of the National government during the first and and third periods. In periods two and four (1939-41 and 1943-44) it found neither praise nor abuse but concern over a possible break in CCP-Kuomintang (KMT) cooperation in the former and reflections of a deteriorating situation in Nationalist China during the latter.

During early 1947 both Kohlberg and the IPR leadership circulated the membership with appeals for proxies. By this point Kohlberg had considerably embellished his charges about Communist influence in the IPR. Finally, on April 22, 1947, the American IPR called to order its special meeting to discuss the charges. Kohlberg took the floor to state that he had witnesses who would say that the Communist party considered the IPR "to be one of its organizations, . . ."[23] Arthur Dean, who chaired the meeting for the institute, avoided this point—as the IPR had ignored it previously. Dean said that he and the other trustees had gone over the charges carefully and found them to be unsubstantiated. The proxies were

22. *An Analysis of Mr. Alfred E. Kohlberg's Charges against the Institute of Pacific Relations* (New York, 1945), p. iii.

23. "Special Meeting of the American Institute of Pacific Relations, Inc., April 22, 1947," p. 12, Columbia Files.

then opened and Kohlberg was defeated by 1,163-66.[24]
Kohlberg then resigned from the IPR and devoted most of
his subsequent efforts to attacks on United States China
policy, rather than the institute *per se.*

Kohlberg's decisive defeat in the 1947 proxy fight was not
an expression of confidence in the IPR leadership. At least an
important minority of the American members were uneasy
about Edward Carter's leadership and desired greater membership control over the New York office. They were repelled,
however, by the indiscriminate nature of Kohlberg's charges
and distrustful of his ever-widening allegations. Had he
limited himself to carefully documented expressions of concern about the quality of IPR leadership and the objectivity
of its publications, Kohlberg might have performed a real
service to both the IPR and United States Asian studies. As
it was, he merely intensified divisions within the IPR, while
at the same time he made it much easier for the IPR leadership to avoid any searching inquiry into the institute's real
problems.[25]

If Kohlberg was defeated, however, he had taken a bit of
the gloss off the institute's image. Contributions slowed, and
not long after the proxy struggle was over, the American IPR
was forced to secure a ten-thousand-dollar loan from the
Pacific Council in order to keep its head above water.[26] It was
the beginning of a series of financial crises for the IPR.

CHINA POLICY AND THE IPR

Clearly, the initial charges of communism and procommunism against the IPR coincided with reports of corruption in

24. Ibid., p. 15

25. Another recent student of the IPR has concluded that a majority
of IPR members would have favored an investigation. See Thomas
Carpenter, "The Institute of Pacific Relations," (Ph.D. diss., Fletcher
School of Law and Diplomacy, Tufts University, 1968), p. 44.

The point is, however, what type of investigation? It is doubtful
if the IPR membership would have favored an investigation of the
Kohlberg charges, especially by those proposed by Kohlberg. Although
this cannot be established from the IPR files, the author believes a
majority might well have approved an inquiry into the quality of IPR
leadership and the objectivity of its publications conducted by persons
devoted to the preservation of an IPR and qualified to judge the
materials presented to them.

26. Carter to Percy Corbett, July 16, 1947, Columbia Files.

the Chinese Government and a deterioration of its military position against the Japanese invaders. Few who charged communism in the IPR were interested in the institute *per se*. What did interest them was the fate of the Nationalist government and United States policy toward China. Such charges were renewed and gained greater frequency as Japan was defeated and it became evident that a greatly strengthened Chinese Communist party posed a significant threat to a united China under Nationalist control. In view of the linkage between China policy and attacks on the IPR, it is appropriate at this point to discuss briefly the evolution of United States policy toward China up to the 1945-47 period.

From the beginning of the KMT-CCP united front against Japan in 1937, the Chinese Communists had moved vigorously to increase their strength for a postwar struggle for power in China. While the war sapped Nationalist strength, it was a boon to the Communists, whose experience as hardy guerrillas and simple administrators was ideally suited to the chaos of war. By the time of Japan's surrender, the Communist base areas were intact and the CCP had secured control of a large part of North China.

United States postwar planning had envisaged a strong, united, and independent China which would be given a substantial position among the world powers.[27] On the other hand, at no time did United States leaders think seriously about significant military involvement in China as a means of influencing such a political outcome. The result was that United States officials saw little choice but to work for unity between the Communists and the Nationalists. At first few people disputed this broad framework of policy.

Ambassador Patrick Hurley, who arrived in China in September 1944, was an enthusiastic supporter of this notion. On the basis of two important, but misguided, assumptions Hurley thought that unity could be achieved within a framework of strong support for the Nationalist government. These were: (1) an inflated view of Nationalist strength; (2) the idea that since the USSR supported President Chiang,

27. This account is based on Tang Tsou, *America's Failure in China, 1941-50* (Chicago: University of Chicago Press, 1963).

the Chinese Communists would ultimately have to accept Chiang's terms. He quickly quarreled with several United States Foreign Service officers in China who had a much less sanguine view of Nationalist prospects and who had proposed that American aid be used as a bargaining tool for reforms in the Central Government.

By the latter part of 1945 it became apparent that Hurley's assumptions were false. The Soviets, despite their willingness to sign the Sino-Soviet Treaty of 1945, as well as other agreements promising support for the National government, withdrew their forces from Manchuria in a manner designed to assist CCP control of the area. Likewise, the Chinese Communists were showing no signs of willingness to accept unity on Nationalist terms. In addition, Washington was moving slowly toward the idea of placing greater pressure on Chiang to come to a political settlement with the Communists. On November 26, Hurley resigned with a blast against unnamed Foreign Service officers for undermining his policy and of siding with "the Chinese Communist armed party."[28] Characteristically, Hurley's statement was filled with the same sort of inconsistencies which had contributed to his failure in China. However, his remarks were of significance to the IPR in that the first time, a well-known government official had embraced the conspiracy theory of American policy toward China. His allegations were also the first public charges raised against the State Department's China specialists.

For a number of reasons, however, Hurley's charges that Americans were giving comfort to the Chinese Communists did not spark a strong response either in Congress or among the public. In part, this was owing to the lack of any sense of crisis about developments in China by late 1945. Although the Nationalists had suffered some setbacks, few thought that Communists would control China within a few short years. In addition, the White House took the play away from its critics by appointing the distinguished general, George Marshall, as Special Presidential Representative in

28. *The China White Paper* (1949) (Stanford, Calif.: Stanford University Press, 1967), p. 581.

China. As long as the Marshall Mission continued, relatively few Americans were disposed to mirror Hurley's charges; relatively few politicians saw great profit in playing up the China issue.

THE FADING OF BIPARTISANSHIP

The failure of the Marshall Mission in January 1947 and the rapidly deteriorating position of the Nationalist government slowly reversed this trend. From 1947 onward China became an increasingly contentious issue in American politics. In part, this development can be attributed to a failure of the Democratic administration to seek active Republican cooperation for its China policy. Thus, many GOP legislators felt little responsibility for the policy and felt few obstacles toward making China a partisan issue. This breakdown in bipartisanship was especially serious in view of the fact that the Republicans, and notably the generally conservative Midwestern Republicans, had long had an interest in China because of the commercial and missionary interests of their constituents.[29] The failure to gain the support of the conservative Republicans was critical, since their constituents, along with those of the antiadministration Southern Democrats, were more susceptible to believing charges of treason and disloyalty over China. Had Governor Dewey vindicated the polls and won the presidency in 1948, perhaps bipartisanship might have returned to China policy. As it was, some Congressional Republicans were suspicious of further bipartisanship in foreign affairs. When the Nationalist collapse occurred, many Republicans in Congress saw no need to muffle their criticism of the administration's China policy.[30]

Not until the fall of the Nationalist government in 1949 did the China policy debate in Congress thoroughly involve the IPR. In 1947 Congressman Walter Judd, a persistent Republican critic of the administration's Far East policies, asked for an investigation of the IPR by the House Committee on Un-American Activities.[31] Judd's suggestion was not taken up.

29. H. Bradford Westerfield, *Foreign Policy and Party Politics* (New Haven, Conn.: Yale University Press, 1955), pp. 240-47.

30. Ibid., pp. 325, 343.

31. *Washington Post*, March 13, 1947.

At the state level, however, there were more ominous signs. A citizen in Glendale, California, wrote State Senator Jack B. Tenney, head of the California Fact-Finding Committee on Un-American Activities, to complain that "Land of the Soviets," an IPR pamphlet used in Glendale schools, contained "pro-Soviet" and "pro-Communist" material.[32] The pamphlet was quickly removed from the Glendale school system,[33] but the matter did not stop there. Senator Tenney's interest in "Land of the Soviets" led him to a sketchy look at the IPR, which he duly included among a series of "Communist and Communist-front organizations" noted by his committee.[34] By itself the incident probably did not result in great damage to the IPR. However, it was a clear sign that the institute would not emerge unscathed from the atmosphere of distrust and suspicion in America emanating from the emerging Cold War.

THE CHINA LOBBY

During the early fifties it became fashionable in the press and in academia to explain the gradual hardening of American policy toward the Chinese Communists in terms of the machinations of a small and secretive "China Lobby" closely aligned with the Chinese Embassy. *The Reporter* magazine devoted two special issues to the subject and painted a stark picture of Nationalist Chinese representatives deliberately spreading the conspiratorial theory of American foreign policy in order to embarrass the administration and to secure more aid for Nationalist China.[35] The theory of the "China Lobby" was developed in much more detail later by Ross Koen in his book, *The China Lobby in American Politics*.[36]

It can be questioned whether the phrase, "China Lobby," best characterizes the phenomenon of growing Congressional

32. *Glendale* (Calif.) *News-Press*, February 19, 1947.
33. *Los Angeles Herald and Express*, March 19, 1947.
34. California, Senate, Fact-Finding Committee on Un-American Activities, *Fourth Report* (Sacramento: 1948), p. 168.
35. Philip Horton, "The China Lobby: Part II," *Reporter*, 6 (April 29, 1952), 5-9
36. Ross Y. Koen, *The China Lobby in American Politics* (New York: Macmillan, 1960). The book was later withdrawn from circulation as a result of a dispute between the author and the publisher.

and public opposition to the administration's China policy during the later forties and early fifties. Certainly it was not a "lobby" in the sense of a united, centralized group subject to direction by the Chinese Embassy. Men such as Patrick Hurley, William Bullitt, Pat McCarran, and Alfred Kohlberg did not necessarily see eye-to-eye beyond their common feeling that the United States should increase its aid to Chiang. Neither were they individuals who easily accepted central direction, whether from Americans or Chinese diplomats. Alfred Kohlberg, although he helped establish the American China Policy Association and the journal, *Plain Talk*, concentrated most of his energies into individual letter-writing. It was the latter activities, rather than the former, which ultimately resulted in grave damage to the IPR.

Efforts to characterize the American supporters of Chiang as a "China Lobby" often miss the mark. Far more important for America's China policy and the IPR was the largely successful effort of an important segment of those favoring Chiang to change the nature of the debate from foreign policy questions to ones involving loyalty and security. In this process, those favoring greater aid to Chiang often accused their opponents of a new and vague sort of disloyalty. As Freda Utley explained it:

Whether in each case such a policy was pursued out of personal ambition, ignorance of the true aims and purpose of the Chinese Communists, or treasonable devotion to their cause, the effect is the same. Those who manipulate the policies of their own government consciously or unconsciously for the benefit of a foreign power by misinforming their own people are more dangerous than spies, even though legally they are not guilty of treason.[37]

In such a fashion did some American supporters of Chiang seek to divert public discussion away from the defects of the National government and the possible problems of a greater United States military involvement in China. Instead, the issue more and more became the loyalty and security practices of those making and implementing United States policy.

One incident which aided those seeking to focus the issue on loyalty and security was the *Amerasia* affair of 1945. On June 6, FBI agents arrested Philip Jaffe, the editor of

37. Freda Utley, *The China Story* (Chicago: Regnery, 1951), p. 124.

Amerasia; Andrew Roth, a Naval Intelligence officer; journalist Mark Gayn; Foreign Service officer John Stewart Service; State Department researcher Emmanuel Larsen; and Kate Mitchell, a former IPR staff member. All were charged with violations of the Espionage Act as a result of extensive FBI surveillance following a search—performed without a warrant—of the *Amerasia* offices several months earlier by agents of the Office of Strategic Services. The agents found hundreds of government documents, some classified as high as Top Secret.

A grand jury found insufficient evidence to indict Mitchell, Service, or Gayn. Because the Justice Department feared that lawyers for Jaffe or Larsen would move to quash their indictments on grounds that evidence had been obtained from an illegal search, it allowed them to plead *nolo contendere* to charges of unauthorized possession of government documents. In court no mention was made of Jaffe's substantial contacts with American Communists. Jaffe was fined two thousand dollars and Larsen five hundred. Charges against Roth were dropped for lack of evidence.[38]

It now appears probable that relatively few of the documents secured by Jaffe were of a sensitive nature. In addition, no evidence was developed by the FBI establishing that government documents had in fact been passed on to foreign powers. Probably the most that could be legitimately concluded from the *Amerasia* affair was that government security practices were very shoddy and that one State Department official had been guilty of a significant lapse in judgment.[39] Nevertheless, the press accounts were subject to easy distortion, especially since the exact nature of the documents was not publicly known. The announcement that a prominent member of the China Service (John Service) had been arrested and that numerous government documents had been leaked

38. U.S., Congress, Senate, Committee on Foreign Relations, Subcommittee Pursuant to S. Resolution 23, *Hearings on the State Department Employee Loyalty Investigation*, 81st Cong., 2d sess., 1950, pp. 923-40, 972-86 (hereafter cited as *Tydings Hearings*).

39. Jaffe later denied that any espionage was involved; see David J. Dallin, *Soviet Espionage* (New Haven, Conn.: Yale University Press, 1955), p. 447.

John Stewart Service's inclusion among the "Amerasia Six" and

was inviting material for those who wished to demonstrate conspiracy in United States policy toward China.

The charges against Philip Jaffe were especially important in view of the close ties which existed between the IPR and *Amerasia*. Several IPR staff members, including Frederick Field, were instrumental in *Amerasia*'s birth. Several others, such as William Lockwood, Owen Lattimore, and T. A. Bisson, served on the *Amerasia* editorial board. For many years the *Amerasia* offices were adjacent to or in the same building as those occupied by the IPR. It was therefore not difficult for critics to tar both with the same brush.[40]

THE SPLIT AMONG FAR EASTERN SCHOLARS

Probably no event has had a more traumatic impact on America's Asian scholars than the victory of the Chinese Communist party in China. By the early 1950's a small but vocal number of Asian specialists were strongly critical of

his subsequent treatment by the State Department are reflective of the "security mania" present in American government during the late forties and early fifties. The grand jury refused unanimously to indict Service by a vote of 20-0. However, in 1951 he was discharged by the State Department on grounds of doubtful loyalty—an action later voided by court action.

What involved Service in the *Amerasia* affair was that he gave Philip Jaffe "8 or 10" personal copies of memoranda he had drafted while attached to the American military mission in Yenan. Service today admits that this action was "unwise and indiscreet," although a common practice at the time. See John Stewart Service, *The Amerasia Papers: Some Problems in the History of U.S.-China Relations.* (Berkeley: Center for Chinese Studies, University of California, 1971), p. 28.

With the advantage of hindsight, it seems clear that Service's treatment by the government was entirely out of proportion to the actions he had taken.

40. Another group with which the IPR was later bracketed by opponents was the Committee for a Democratic Far Eastern Policy (CDFEP). According to testimony provided by Max Yergan, the CDFEP was organized at a meeting at Frederick Field's home. Yergan testified that Field told him he was being invited to the founding meeting at the instruction of Communist party chief Eugene Dennis. See *McCarran Hearings*, pp. 4595-4601. Although the CDFEP contained non-Communist figures such as IPR staffers Maxwell Stewart and his wife, it functioned as a party-dominated organization. By 1950 the CDFEP had made clear its open support for the Chinese Communists.

what had seemed like generally accepted scholarship on China and American policy in Asia. In the process several warm friends of the thirties became bitter enemies by the late forties or early fifties.

Of course, events in China did not cause the deep divisions among Asian scholars which were evident by the early 1950's. They merely intensified and brought into the open some basic disagreements about China and political analysis which very likely had existed for some time. A recent analysis has traced these divisions to differing conceptions of the nature of man, the modernization process, and revolutionary change.[41] "Liberals" viewed the common man as able to choose his own destiny. They thus saw events in China more in terms of a revolutionary process in which the Communists were demonstrating significant abilities to enlist the active support of the people. They saw little opportunity for the West to intervene directly in China, and tended to downplay the international significance of a CCP victory.

"Conservative" scholars, on the other hand, doubted the capacity of the common man in China to see his own best interests. They thus described reflections of popular support for the CCP mainly in terms of organization and indoctrination. Seeing the Chinese civil war mainly as a struggle for power to be decided by military forces, they considered the actions of foreign powers to be quite important. In addition, they saw the outcome in China as significant for the global struggle between communism and democracy, and doubted the possibility of changes which might modify Chinese Communist hostility for the United States.[42] These latter beliefs probably influenced a relatively few "conservative" scholars to question the motives of those who did not share the extent of their concern. In any event, the IPR, as the principal Asian studies organization, could not escape the new divisiveness among Asian scholars.

One factor which likely fueled growing divisions among Asian scholars during the 1940's was a series of controversial books on the Asian scene and United States policy by Owen

41. Ben Lee Martin, "Interpretations of United States Policy toward the Chinese Communists, 1944-1968: Survey and Analysis," (Ph.D. diss., Fletcher School of Law and Diplomacy, Tufts University, 1968).

42. Ibid., pp. 7-10, 131-33.

Lattimore. Although hardly a specialist on either international relations or Asian politics, Lattimore plunged into his task with characteristic aplomb. The results, especially when viewed with the advantage of hindsight, reveal Lattimore's many limitations as a writer on international politics. Terms such as "democracy" and "feudal" were often employed without careful definition; sweeping generalizations about the thinking of Asian "peoples" commonly appeared with little documentation. Particularly glaring was the absence of any expressed appreciation for the role of power in international affairs. Thus, Lattimore could describe Outer Mongolia as "a satellite of Russia in the good sense; that is to say, the Mongols have gravitated into the Russian orbit of their own accord (and partly out of fear of Japan and China)."[43]

Especially important for Lattimore (and the IPR, since he had played an important role in it) was his failure to define clearly his attitude toward possible gains by Communists or the Soviet Union in Asia. At one point, Lattimore claimed that Soviet policy toward Mongolia was a "standard with which other nations must compete if they wish to practice a policy of attraction in Asia."[44] At another he asserted that "America has at present the clearest power of attraction for all Asia."[45] To a critic who had apparently asked him to clarify his viewpoint, Lattimore replied that "the American interest, *of course*, is that Communism should spread as little as possible. The only question is how to do it. The present American policy in China should be changed, not because it is anti-Communist, but because it is unsuccessfully anti-Communist."[46] Such an approach did not come through clearly in his books, however.

An additional factor in the controversy, and one which probably embittered relations between "conservatives" and "liberals" in the Asian field, was the tardiness of the "conservatives" in expressing clear-cut differences on China policy. Not until 1948 or 1949, when the issue had been largely

43. Owen Lattimore, *Solution in Asia* (Boston: Little, Brown, and Co., 1945), p. 142.
44. Ibid., p. 144.
45. Ibid., p. 152.
46. Lattimore to Elbert D. Thomas, June 10, 1948, Columbia Files.

resolved, did "conservatives" begin to speak up publicly and question some previously dominant attitudes in academic thinking about America's China policy. In part, this absence of public comment may have resulted from the fact that many Far Eastern scholars were employed by the government during wartime. Thus, disputes over China policy were argued out privately within the administration.[47] Even if one grants this view, however, it is difficult to explain why there was so little "conservative" critique from academic sources of American China policy during the key years of 1946 and 1947. It is difficult to avoid the hypothesis that many "conservative" China scholars were tardy in appreciating the rapidity of Nationalist collapse and gave full expression to their views only when the situation had gravely deteriorated. The timing of "conservative" criticism was especially unfortunate, since it fed "liberal" fears that the "conservatives" were swaying with the tides of popular opinion rather than reinterpreting the data about the significance of the Chinese civil war. Their fears were intensified by the occasional willingness of some "conservatives" to impute "procommunism" to the views of some well-known "liberal" scholars.

THE IPR AND THE ASIAN CRISIS

In view of the dramatic events taking place in Asia and the tensions building up in America over our China policy, the period between 1944 and 1949 was to provide severe tests for the IPR. The remainder of this chapter will focus on the institute's response, especially as it was manifested in publications policy, continued regionalism, and handling of internal criticism.

Publications

As previously noted, during the first two decades of the IPR, *Pacific Affairs*, the journal of the International IPR, generally took a more controversial approach to East Asian political questions than its sister publication, *Far Eastern Survey*. Between 1944 and 1949, however, this pattern was reversed. Again, the new pattern was not the result of policy

47. I am indebted to Professor George Taylor for suggesting this point.

considerations by either the AIPR trustees or the Pacific Council. Personalities were the key factor.

Philip Lilienthal, editor of *Pacific Affairs* for most of the period under review, did not differ personally with those who were critical of the Nationalist government or of United States policy.[48] However, he lacked the same assurance about East Asian developments that had impelled Owen Lattimore to speak out so strongly. As a result, *Pacific Affairs* demonstrated a good deal more balance and far less flamboyance than it had during the Lattimore days. Authors utilized by Lilienthal were less controversial, and there was little of the anonymous authorship sometimes permitted by Lattimore. Generally speaking, readers of *Pacific Affairs* found no sense of urgency about Asian developments or United States China policy.

On the few occasions when *Pacific Affairs* under Lilienthal did venture into Chinese political issues, it did so with caution. In the March 1946 issue Sir Frederick Whyte assessed the Chinese scene. Whyte wrote that the Chinese Communist movement was essentially a "potent agrarian opposition."[49] He failed to indicate any real degree of crisis or to delineate any policy options for the United States, however. Two years later, Frank Lee discussed land reforms in the Communist area.[50] Lee left no suggestion that the authors of the reforms were anything other than Communists. In an editorial note, Lilienthal warned his readers that the article was based heavily on Communist sources.

Not until December 1948, when the Nationalist position was grave, did *Pacific Affairs* venture into the touchy subject of United States China policy. The task was entrusted to D. B. Copland, a former Australian ambassador to China. Copland criticized United States policy for excessive identification with the Nationalists, but he also quoted United States officials who were concerned about "the inability of the

48. Philip Lilienthal, personal interview, July 8, 1970.
49. Sir Frederick Whyte, "Chungking or Yenan," *Pacific Affairs*, 19 (March 1946): 201.
50. Frank C. Lee, "Land Redistribution in Communist China," *Pacific Affairs*, 21 (March 1948): 20-32.

Chinese Government to combat the menace of the Communists. . . ."[51]

Laurence Salisbury, the editor of *Far Eastern Survey* during much of the 1944-49 period, suffered from none of Lilienthal's lack of sureness about the Chinese scene. A retired Foreign Service officer who had served in China, Salisbury had very definite ideas about Chinese politics and United States policy, and pushed his views in *Far Eastern Survey*. The result was that the *Survey* dealt far more extensively and far more controversially with the increasingly contentious Chinese political scene.

By late 1944 the *Survey* began to summarize news reports about the significance of General Joseph Stillwell's resignation as well as reports citing inefficiency or corruption in the National government. Editor Salisbury stressed that the "Communist" areas (for which he invariably used quotation marks) were "in fact primarily agrarian communities intent on driving the Japanese from China."[52]

Although Salisbury often balanced articles critical of the KMT with more favorable accounts by authors such as David Rowe and Lin Yu-Tang, the *Survey*'s partisanship was evident in lead articles—indistinguishable from editorials—by the editor. By the spring of 1945 Salisbury was castigating Washton for supporting a "repressive oligarchy" in China.[53] By late 1947 the editors were making a sharp rejoinder to William Bullitt's proposal that the United States lend the Chinese government $1.35 billion to make internal reforms and to eliminate the CCP. Contrary assessments of the Chinese scene and United States policy were given by Franz Michael and Paul M. A. Linebarger, but it was clear that the *Survey*'s editors were not neutral on such issues.

Salisbury's outspoken position did not go unnoticed by his readers, several of whom wrote in to protest his editorial practices. Increased criticism of the *Survey* came to a head

51. D. B. Copland, "United States Policy in China," *Pacific Affairs*, 21 (December 1948): 345.

52. *Far Eastern Survey*, 13 (November 14, 1944): 2.

53. Laurence E. Salisbury, "Our China Policy," *Far Eastern Survey*, 13 (April 25, 1945): 89.

in 1945 with the resignation of an AIPR Executive Committee member. The member was particularly concerned over one article which he had considered unscholarly.[54] Edward Carter strongly supported Salisbury, telling the Executive Committee that it should not crumble under criticism or act in fear of Kohlberg and the Hearst press. As so often happened, Carter carried the day and Salisbury was retained as editor. It was an example of Edward Carter's extraordinary ability to influence men, especially those on the AIPR Executive Committee. It also demonstrated how Carter was able to use the Kohlberg charges as a means of avoiding action on important academic questions facing the IPR. On some occasions, Kohlberg was more of a help than a hindrance to Edward Carter.

Despite the support of Carter, Laurence Salisbury apparently was not satisfied. He remained as editor until November 1947, when he resigned, citing his irritation over efforts by the Executive Committee to force him to use only "balanced" or "non-controversial" material in the *Survey*.[55]

Regionalism Renewed

The previous chapter has examined the strong regional tendencies which existed in the American Institute of Pacific Relations. Prior to 1944, these divisions had been manageable; despite their concern and criticism, influential members of the San Francisco, Seattle, and Hawaii chapters remained in the IPR. The beginnings of the Cold War in America shattered this surface calm, however, and brought the issue to a head.

West Coast concern over the leadership of the New York office was exacerbated during the Hot Springs Conference of 1945. Several Northwest members were incensed by what they considered staff domination of the American delegation at Hot Springs.[56] As a result a Northwest trustee tried to negotiate the matter privately with AIPR Secretary Raymond Dennett. The trustee hoped that the matter could be alleviated by giving greater autonomy to regional units.

54. Carpenter, "The Institute of Pacific Relations," p. 137.
55. Salisbury to Carter, November 18, 1947, Columbia Files.
56. Circular letter from Charles E. Martin to the Board of Trustees, February 11, 1946, McLaughlin Papers.

The New York office outwardly demonstrated some signs of sensitivity to the desires for greater regional autonomy. The matter was explored in the 1944-46 biennial report of the AIPR. Various efforts were made to revise voting regulations so that West Coast AIPR members could have more say in selecting trustees who would represent their viewpoints. Finally, it was decided to hold a special meeting of the AIPR in April 1947 to consider various methods for resolving regional conflicts in the IPR.

In the meantime the conflicts sharpened. A particular sore point with the San Francisco Chapter was the continued retention of Frederick Field on the Executive Committee, despite his increasingly open adherence to Communist causes. In early 1946 an important San Francisco official, Admiral John W. Greenslade, wrote Carter to complain about some of Field's recent writings about China for the *Daily Worker* and the *New Masses*. Greenslade thought that Field's position on the Board of Trustees was a threat to the fundamental purposes of the American Council. He suggested that Field be asked to choose between a search for truth and the propagation of dogmas.[57] Carter's reply defended Field's presence on the board in terms of upholding the principle of freedom of opinion and expression.[58]

Greenslade's proposal was not taken up, and the pressures from San Francisco and also from Seattle for Field's ouster intensified. These efforts did not result from beliefs that Field was influencing the IPR toward objectives of the Communist party or that Field was the focal point of a communist cell in the IPR. Rather, institute leaders on the West Coast were finding it increasingly difficult to explain Field's presence on the board to their friends and especially to financial contributors. These difficulties mounted with the Soviet-American rift and the increasing presence of strong Cold War beliefs among the public.

As early as January 1946 the San Francisco IPR leaders had considered the idea of merging their chapter into an enlarged World Affairs Council as one method of solving their

57. John W. Greenslade to Carter, February 27, 1946, Hoover Files.
58. Carter to Greenslade, March 1, 1946, Columbia Files.

persistent problems with the New York office.[59] No final decisions were taken in that year, but by early 1947 the matter had reached a crisis stage. In January of that year the San Francisco Executive Committee received a report from three of its members that fund raising for the San Francisco IPR had become very difficult because of charges of Communist influence in the head office.[60] These difficulties were likely assisted by an anonymous memorandum to that effect which circulated in San Francisco during 1947.[61]

Apparently believing that strong action would have to be taken to save the IPR in San Francisco, the Bay Region Executive Committee passed a motion saying that IPR interests would be best served if Frederick Field and Edward Carter were no longer connected with the IPR.[62] The motion was supported by the Seattle chapter, which was operating under similar pressures and shared the distrust of the San Francisco leaders for the New York office. Thus were disputes of very long standing in the IPR finally brought to a head for decision by the Board of Trustees, nominally the chief policy-making body of the AIPR.

How the board handled the matter was an excellent indication of power and influence within the IPR. When it met to consider the matter on March 18, 1947, only about one third of the trustees were in attendance. No West Coast members were present to argue their case. Those attending were generally those eastern trustees over whom Edward Carter had long exercised considerable influence. In debating the question most of the trustees expressed the view that Field had been a valuable and objective member and should be retained. They argued that his removal would seem like a concession to Kohlberg; it was also noted that Field had received a majority of votes even from the San Francisco members in the last Trustee election. Apparently no mention was made of the damage which Field's name had brought to the San Francisco IPR and the fact that the very existence of the San Fran-

59. San Francisco IPR, Minutes of Committee on Policy and Organizational Development Meeting, January 29, 1946, Hoover Files.

61. For this information I am indebted to Mrs. Frank Gerbode, who has provided me with a copy of the memorandum.

62. San Francisco IPR, Minutes of Executive Committee Meeting, January 14, 1947.

cisco group might be at stake. Field was then retained on the board by a vote of 14-1.[63]

The board's decision was a strong impetus to the San Francisco leaders to realize their desire to establish a World Affairs Council. Before that decision was announced to the San Francisco members, however, the AIPR's long-awaited special meeting was held at Coronado, California, April 9-13. Far from healing the breach between the West Coast members and New York, the meeting merely confirmed West Coast suspicions that Edward Carter had no intention of heeding their protests.

The delegates at Coronado, many of whom were from the West Coast, adopted two resolutions. The first urged the Board of Trustees to explore the possibility of union or greater cooperation with other organizations involved in international affairs; the second declared that the first should not prevent prompt consideration of union or some form of joint organization between the IPR and the Foreign Policy Association, the latter a nonprofit American organization concerned with education and research in American foreign policy.[64] The whole tenor of the discussion, of course, reflected the distrust which important West Coast members had long felt for the IPR's national leadership.

As far as can be determined from the written record, Edward Carter at first attempted to sidetrack the discussion of the Coronado resolutions; when he perceived the strong feelings of the delegates he gave an impression of support. However, in reviewing the proceedings for the entire AIPR membership, Carter gave an account which several West Coast leaders considered very misleading.[65] There is no evidence from the IPR files to suggest that either Carter or the Board of Trustees gave serious consideration to the Coronado resolutions. Only several years later, when the

63. AIPR, Minutes of Board of Trustees Meeting, March 18, 1947, Hoover Files.

64. San Francisco IPR, "Report to the Members of the Bay Region IPR on the First National Conference of the American IPR held at Coronado, California, April 9-13, 1947," Hoover Files.

65. See Eugene Staley to Philip Jessup, May 3, 1947, Hoover Files; Lynn White, Jr., to Mary C. Wright, September 18, 1950, McLaughlin Papers.

IPR's very existence seemed at stake, did high institute leaders carefully consider such a course.

As for Frederick Field, not even the decision of the San Francisco IPR leaders to set up a World Affairs Council of Northern California in April 1947 was sufficient to effect his removal from the board. Only in July, after the closure of the Southern California IPR office, was pressure placed on Field to offer his resignation. He did so in late July in a letter which decried the fact that the IPR was giving in to financial pressures by removing him.[66]

The tardiness of the national IPR leaders to react to the concerns of regional officials in part resulted from a slowness to grasp the significance of changes in the American political environment for the future of the IPR. In 1944 few if any institute leaders thought that the Kohlberg charges would cause serious damage; they were very wrong. In similar fashion, they failed in 1946-47 to see that rapid changes in the American political climate might threaten the continuance of regional IPR units and ultimately the whole IPR. As a result, by 1948 the institute no longer had chapters in San Francisco and Seattle, two of its strongholds on the West Coast.

A Leadership under Fire

As 1947 wore on, Edward Carter's position as executive secretary of the American IPR became increasingly vulnerable. Although he had been responsible for much of the IPR's growth, now he was becoming a distinct liability within America's changed political climate. Two incidents in 1947 illustrated Carter's unwillingness to make any substantial modifications in his outside activities which could reflect adversely on the IPR. The first involved *The Unfinished Revolution in China*, a book by Israel Epstein. Although Epstein's work was essentially a paean to the Chinese Communists, Carter was much impressed and inclined to accept Epstein's request that the IPR promote the book. Despite William Holland's suggestion that he be "a little less unqualified in [his] enthusiasm" because of the book's "pretty clear bias," Carter proceeded to write a number of friends and government officials suggesting that they read *Unfinished Revolution*

66. Field to Carter, July 23, 1947, McLaughlin Papers.

in China.[67] In a separate incident, Carter showed how little
he had responded to West Coast criticism by informing a
prominent member of the San Francisco IPR that he had
given the proceedings of the 1947 Stratford-on-Avon Conference to Soviet officials.[68]

Finally in 1948 Edward Carter was persuaded to retire and
Clayton Lane was selected as executive secretary of the
American IPR. Lane believed his task to be one of restoring
confidence in the IPR. To achieve such a goal, he was willing
to be a good bit more conciliatory than previous AIPR secre-
taries to those who either were attacking the institute or were
concerned about charges of Communist infiltration. Faced
with the conflicting judgments of the Executive Committee,
the Pacific Coast trustees, and the staff, however, Lane found
this to be an unattainable task. The staff wanted to keep things
as they were; several trustees wanted significant changes in
staff and administration; and the Executive Committee
wanted him to set a new course while at the same time defending Edward Carter's previous actions.[69]

Just how difficult it was to conciliate all factions is shown
by two incidents which took place during Clayton Lane's
tenure as secretary of the AIPR. In 1948 the AIPR was
considering the appointment of Lawrence Rosinger to its
research staff. A prominent West Coast member wrote in to
oppose the nomination. Although Rosinger was not charged
with Communist connections, apparently someone had com-
pared his writings to those of the Communists and saw enough
parallels to question his objectivity.[70] Rosinger defended his
independence of judgment and the Executive Committee
voted to support his nomination.

A more difficult case was posed by materials submitted by
Abraham Chapman, a writer on Philippine politics. The
dispute began in 1949 when Chapman submitted an article
for *Far Eastern Survey.* Clayton Lane opposed publication
because Chapman was a member of the Executive Committee
of the Committee for a Democratic Far Eastern Policy,

67. Holland to Carter, June 12, 1947, Columbia Files.
68. Mrs. Frank Gerbode, personal interview, June 15, 1970.
69. Clayton Lane to Arthur H. Dean undated, Columbia Files.
70. William L. Holland, personal interview, March 18, 1970.

which had been listed as subversive by the Attorney General. Lane argued that the IPR should not accept papers by enemies of free inquiry and that acceptance would damage the reputation of the institute and hurt its fund-raising efforts. Staff member Miriam Farley strongly disagreed and argued that the manuscript itself, not the author's political beliefs, should be the governing factor. The Executive Committee agreed, but not unanimously, to withhold publication.[71]

The next year, Chapman's name again figured in an IPR controversy. On this occasion the question was whether the institute should publish his manuscript, "Philippine Nationalism," which had been scheduled for printing that year by the International Secretariat. By this time, Chapman had admitted to William Holland that he was a member of the Communist party.[72] After the IPR received a strenuous objection from the Pacific Northwest Division, Chapman's book was not published.

By the middle of 1950, it was apparent that Clayton Lane would not be able to bring together the AIPR's divergent elements. He resigned, saying he had failed in his purpose of restoring confidence in the IPR.[73] William Holland was then asked to take over the AIPR secretary's position in addition to his main job as secretary-general of the IPR

Thus, as the IPR entered the 1950's, it had been severely weakened as a regional American force by the charges begun by Alfred Kohlberg in 1944. Of particular importance was that Kohlberg and others attacking the IPR were able to alter the nature of criticism from essentially academic grounds to those of security and loyalty. In raising these new issues, they infinitely complicated the task of the IPR's internal critics, who wanted to preserve the organization, but who hoped for less controversial leadership and more balanced coverage of the Asian scene.

71. Minutes of Executive and Finance Committees, January 11, 1950 —"Confidential," Columbia Files. For further information about the Committee for a Democratic Far Eastern Policy, please see Note 40, above in this chapter.

72. Pacific Northwest Division, Minutes of Executive Committee Meeting, July 12, 1950, Columbia Files.

73. "Announcement to Members of the American Institute of Pacific Relations," undated, Columbia Files.

Despite his vigorous efforts, Alfred Kohlberg was unable to focus the spotlight of national publicity on the IPR during the 1940's. But very soon other men were to bring Kohlberg's charges onto the national level and to imperil the very existence of the IPR. That episode will be examined next.

3

McCarthy and Tydings:
A Shift to the National Scene

JUST as the IPR was beginning to catch its breath after the damage to its regional structure, the whirlwind struck. The McCarthy period had begun with an emotionalism that made reasoned discourse about East Asia very difficult. Government personnel were the first to feel the heat of the new pressures for conformity, but writers and academics were quickly to follow. Within two years, the IPR was struggling for its survival.

THE AMERICAN MOOD AND "McCARTHYISM"

In retrospect it is apparent that many factors were involved in the McCarthy movement. Some explanations for the rise of McCarthyism in America during the early 1950's have stressed historical factors. There is no doubt that such factors played an important role in producing an atmosphere in which the public would be receptive to Senator Joseph McCarthy's charges. During 1948 and 1949, the American people had been confronted with a series of shocking events which increased public fears and anxieties. In 1948, ex-Communists Elizabeth Bentley and Whittaker Chambers came forward with their explosive charges about espionage in the high reaches of government. Additional setbacks came in 1949. In August the Chinese Communist party completed its victory on the Chinese mainland. In September it was announced that the Soviet Union had tested an atomic device—several years ahead of previous estimates. Justice Department staff member Judith Coplon was accused of espionage and Alger Hiss, a senior State Department aide, was indicted for perjury in the courts and for espionage in the popular mind. In the words of historian Eric Goldman, 1949 was truly a "year of shocks."[1] The next year opened with news that Hiss had been convicted.

Historians have also stressed the American public's lack of experience with intractable foreign crises and its misconceptions about the United States role in Asia.[2] It was extremely difficult for many to understand how America's will could not be wrought in China so soon after our smashing victory in World War II.[3] For a short time, events seemed to lend credence to those who charged that hidden conspiracies were the key to United States foreign policy setbacks.

Important as historical factors were to the development of the McCarthy period, social scientists have also suggested some elements which may be more institutional than historical. Both Richard Hofstadter and Eric Goldman assert that high anxiety levels associated with rootlessness and rapid social change produced a good deal of support for Senator McCarthy, who seemed for a moment to be blocking such trends.[4] The persistence of such anxieties almost twenty years later suggests that they are more institutional than

1.   Eric F. Goldman, *The Crucial Decade* (New York: Alfred A. Knopf, 1956), p. 112.

2. See George Davis, "The Dissolution of the Institute of Pacific Relations, 1944-1961" (Ph.D. diss. University of Chicago, 1966), p. 155. Davis' viewpoint might be termed the "adolescent" theory of American foreign policy.

3. In 1952 the British observer Dennis Brogan noted the odd belief of some Americans that the United States "had" a China to "lose"; see "The Illusion of American Omnipotence," *Harper's*, 205 (December 1952): 21-28. How widespread this belief actually was is debatable. However, some of the political rhetoric of the early fifties suggests that important American politicians believed it was widespread.

4. See Richard Hofstadter, *The Paranoid Style in American Politics* (New York: Alfred A. Knopf, 1965), p. 51; Goldman, *The Crucial Decade*, pp. 119-21. The problem, of course, is to determine how deep such anxieties go and whether or not they are subject to exploitation by political leaders. Interpreters of the public's mood at a particular moment can easily overestimate the degree of anxiety felt by the public and hence its response to arguments similar to those of Senator

historical, more understandable in terms of the modern world and contemporary American life than as temporary historical phenomena.

In retrospect, it also seems likely that McCarthy exploited the antagonisms which exist between well-educated, affluent urban America and some segments of rural America. The spectacle of the rough-hewn Senator from Wisconsin dishing it out to "striped-panted snobs" in the State Department was likely welcomed by some who may not have been especially concerned with America's foreign policy problems.[5]

THE SENATOR FROM WISCONSIN

Exactly what Senator Joseph McCarthy said in Wheeling, West Virginia, on February 9, 1950, may never be known. Whatever his exact remarks, however, the American press was soon full of McCarthy's sensational charges about Communists in the State Department. Recognizing the dangers which might follow, the Democratic administration attempted to take the play away from the Wisconsin Republican by agreeing to have his charges immediately investigated by a special subcommittee of the Senate Foreign Relations Committee headed by Senator Millard Tydings of Maryland.

Prior to his appearance before the Tydings Committee, McCarthy had not mentioned prominent individuals connected with the IPR. As soon as he was asked to provide the names of specific cases, however, it became evident that the IPR could not escape McCarthy's fire. On March 21, the press carried reports that he had charged former AIPR trustee Philip Jessup with "an unusual affinity for Communist causes."[6] An even greater shock was provided on March 27, when it became known McCarthy had charged that Owen Lattimore was "the top Russian espionage agent" in the

McCarthy. See Samuel A. Stouffer, *Communism, Conformity, and Civil Liberties* (Garden City, N.Y.: Doubleday, 1955), p. 59.

5. Sociologist Martin Trow found that support for McCarthy was heaviest among small businessmen dissatisfied with trends toward big business, big labor, and big government and lacking ways to channel their dissent; see "Small Businessmen, Political Tolerance, and Support for McCarthy," *American Journal of Sociology*, 64 (November 1958): 273-74.

6. *New York Times*, March 21, 1950.

United States and "one of the top advisers on Far Eastern policy."[7] McCarthy then said he would "stand or fall" on the Lattimore case.[8]

There is no evidence that McCarthy consulted with Alfred Kohlberg or other well-known critics of the IPR before making his charges against Lattimore and Jessup. In late March, however, Kohlberg went to Washington and agreed to furnish McCarthy with material he had previously distributed charging Communist infiltration of the IPR. McCarthy refused Kohlberg's offer of a financial contribution on the grounds that Kohlberg had been connected with the "China Lobby" in the press and he wanted to avoid the notion that his investigation was being financed by such a lobby.[9] After he had received Kohlberg's data, on March 30 McCarthy made a lengthy speech to the Senate in which he detailed his charges of Communist subversion in government and focused his attention on Lattimore and the IPR. The speech included Kohlberg's "four stages" of the Communist line on China.[10]

THE TYDINGS HEARINGS

The Tydings Committee began its hearings on March 8, 1950, with the task of discovering whether or not "disloyal" Americans were being employed by the State Department. From the beginning the committee was plagued by a conflict between its majority and minority members. The Democratic majority, composed of Senator Tydings and Senators Brien McMahon of Connecticut and Theodore Francis Green of Rhode Island, appeared acutely conscious of the political ramifications of the investigation. The Democratic members generally acted as if they desired a quick investigation of Senator McCarthy's evidence and the issuance of a report which would convince their fellow Americans that McCarthy was off target and reassure them about the conduct of American diplomacy. They were often skeptical of witnesses who offered sensational charges of communism and occasionally quite deferential toward those who responded to such charges.

7. Ibid., March 27, 1950
8. Goldman, *The Crucial Decade, p. 143.*
9. Keeley, *The China Lobby Man*, pp. 98-99.
10. *Congressional Record*, (March 30, 1950): 4378-79.

The majority's counsel, Edward Morgan, also reflected these viewpoints.

The minority, composed of Senators Henry Cabot Lodge of Massachusetts and Bourke Hickenlooper of Iowa, was of quite a different mind. Although neither Lodge nor Hickenlooper could be called a partisan of McCarthy, they both desired a thorough investigation of his charges. They were much less inclined to limit the scope of the hearings and, of course, far less concerned about the political implications of the investigation.

The Republicans also selected their own man, Robert Morris, to serve as minority counsel. In a number of ways, it was an unfortunate choice. Although Morris was familiar with Communist and Communist-front activities from his days in Naval Intelligence and his work on the Rapp-Coudert hearings in New York,[11] he was not in any sense an impartial investigator. As he later candidly admitted, he was (and is) a firm believer in the conspiracy theory of America's Far Eastern policy. Long before the Tydings hearings, Morris had come to the conclusion that the IPR was infiltrated with Communists and pressed the committee to look into the "Communist cell" in the institute.[12] As might be expected Morris quickly differed with Majority Counsel Morgan about how the investigation should be conducted, what witnesses should be called, and what evidence should be admitted.[13] However, since the Democrats were in control, the investigation largely proceeded on the basis desired by Senator Tydings. Morris was not able to question witnesses until very late in the hearings, when Senator Lodge demanded that he be allowed to do so.

Despite the aforementioned restrictions, the Tydings hearings nevertheless produced some sensational charges and countercharges which directly involved the IPR. Ex-Communist Louis Budenz, a former foreign editor of the *Daily Worker*, told the committee that there was a Communist cell in the IPR headed by Frederick Field. He also referred to an alleged meeting in 1937, at which Field and Communist

11. The Rapp-Coudert hearings (1940-41) investigated Communist activities in the New York school system.

12. Robert Morris, *No Wonder We Are Losing* (New York: Book-mailer, 1958), pp. 52, 106.

13. Ibid., p. 103.

party chief Earl Browder were said to have discussed Owen Lattimore's efforts in placing Communist writers in the IPR.[14] According to Budenz, these efforts were aimed at promoting the line that the Chinese Communist party was like a group of "North Dakota nonpartisan Leaguers."[15] Budenz further asserted that at a 1943 meeting of party officials, it was reported that Lattimore, through Field, had received word of a change in the Communist line on Chiang Kai-shek. Budenz claimed that the change in line then appeared in the *Far Eastern Survey* as T. A. Bisson's article on "democratic" and "feudal" China.[16]

Of course, a questioner thoroughly familiar with the IPR might have been able to cast considerable doubt on the accuracy of some of Budenz' statements. As previously noted, the "agrarian reformer" concept was not prominently featured in *Pacific Affairs* during Lattimore's editorship; it *was* a common feature of the *Survey* under Laurence Salisbury, but neither Budenz nor any other witness claimed that Salisbury was under Communist direction or influence. In addition, Budenz seemed unaware that Lattimore had left *Pacific Affairs* in 1941, and had no editorial responsibility for either that journal or the *Survey* from then on.[17]

Several of the committee members were concerned, however, that Budenz, despite numerous opportunities to do so, had not previously mentioned Lattimore in either his public writings or his conversations with the FBI. Under intensive questioning he asserted that he had failed to include Lattimore in his reports to the FBI because there were so many people to identify; he had not named him in press articles because of the possibility of libel charges.[18]

Continued questioning by several skeptical senators also elicited two theories which Budenz felt explained some

14. *Tydings Hearings*, pp. 491-92.
15. Ibid., p. 492.
16. Ibid. The implication of Budenz' remarks was that Lattimore had been responsible for the Bisson article. However, he did not specifically state this view, and the matter was left unclarified by the Tydings Committee.
17. Ibid., pp. 518-20.
18. According to Joseph Alsop, in 1947 Budenz told a State Department investigator that he could not recall any concrete actions suggest-

apparent discrepancies in information presented to the committee. The first might be called the theory of exemptions. When Counsel Morgan read him a *Daily Worker* review which strongly criticized Lattimore's *Situation in Asia*, Budenz explained that this practice was often followed to protect hidden party people.[19] Budenz' second explanation can be termed the theory of comradely truth. In essence, it says that while Communist party members often lie to the public, they tell the truth to each other. The theory is vital to the accuracy of Budenz' testimony, since so many of his allegations were based on oral "reports" which he received from higher party officials such as Jack Stachel.

Despite some challenges from the committee, Budenz maintained his position. He testified that in 1944 Stachel had told him to consider Lattimore as a Communist and to treat as authoritative his writings and advice.[20] He also went on to list Edward Carter and Benjamin Kizer, an AIPR trustee, as Communists.[21]

Budenz' statements about Owen Lattimore and the relationship between the IPR and the Communist party were sharply disputed by two other ex-Communist witnesses, Earl Browder and Bella Dodd. A number of difficulties exist in evaluating their testimony, however. Neither had completely broken with communism, although both were no longer members of the party. Dr. Dodd's background really did not qualify her to judge the issues raised by Budenz; ex-Communist party chief Browder's testimony suggests that he either (1) did not desire to tell the committee about the conspiratorial aspects of American communism or (2) was unaware of them. Browder was often unresponsive to the committee, refusing

---

ing that Lattimore was a Communist. In 1949, he told a *Collier's* editor that Lattimore, though "misguided," had never "acted as a Communist in any way." Only after McCarthy's charges were made known did Budenz go to the FBI to charge that Lattimore was a Red. See Joseph Alsop, "The Strange Case of Louis Budenz," *Atlantic Monthly*, 189 (April 1952): 29-33.

19. *Tydings Hearings*, p. 525. Budenz did not say how the party rank-and-file was supposed to distinguish between true enemies and exempted supporters.

20. Ibid., p. 492.

21. Ibid., p. 627.

to answer questions about his associations with a host of individuals named by Counsel Morgan. Browder did, however, name James Allen, an occasional writer for *Pacific Affairs*, as a party member.[22]

Given the opportunity to comment on Budenz' charges at the hearings, Frederick Field invoked his Fifth Amendment privilege against self-incrimination.[23] Owen Lattimore, on the other hand, met the charges head on with a vehemence and intemperance similar to that of his attackers. He was allowed to read into the record a long and harshly worded statement which lashed out at Senator McCarthy and accused Budenz of lying.[24] When he had finished, Counsel Morgan aptly summarized, "You and Senator McCarthy are now even, . . ."[25] Naturally, Lattimore's method of response made hot news. In terms of the impact on the IPR, however, the result was unfortunate, since the public's view of the institute increasingly became intertwined with McCarthy's charge and Lattimore's countercharges.

By the standards of Congressional committees, Lattimore was accorded unusual prerogatives. Not only was he allowed to read his statement into the record with few interruptions; his lawyer, Abe Fortas, was permitted to prepare questions which in effect served to cross-examine witnesses making allegations against his client. The questioning of Lattimore was very polite, at times even deferential, and he was given a full opportunity to explain his position. In his defense, Lattimore said that he had not known James S. Allen as a Communist when he accepted Allen's contributions for *Pacific Affairs*. He also pointed to statements in his books which he said refuted the claim that he had followed the twists and turns of the Communist press with regard to President Chiang Kai-shek.[26]

Lattimore was also the beneficiary of another unusual committee procedure: the oral release of FBI data. During the hearings Senator Tydings mentioned that Lattimore's FBI file had been made available to four members of the

22. Ibid., p. 689.
23. Ibid., p. 710.
24. Ibid., pp. 800-4
25. Ibid., p. 831.
26. Ibid., p. 807.

committee, and they had seen nothing in it to suggest that he
was either a Communist or an espionage agent.[27]

THE TYDINGS REPORT

The conclusions of the Tydings Committee majority members were released on July 20, 1950. Among other things, the committee absolved Lattimore of charges that he had been a spy or had followed the Communist "line." It conceded that in his contacts Lattimore might not have "exercised the discretion which our knowledge of communism in 1950 indicates would have been wise, . . ." However, it found no evidence that he had knowingly associated with Communists. The report also expressed concern that the types of charges being aired against writers such as Lattimore might restrict intellectual freedom. It also exonerated Philip Jessup and praised the IPR.[28] Neither Senator Lodge nor Senator Hickenlooper signed the report. Lodge delivered a statement of his individual views which criticized the limited scope of the investigation and called for a bipartisan commission to study the questions raised in the Tydings hearings.[29]

Of course, the Tydings Committee had in no sense conducted an investigation of the IPR. It had taken some testimony about the institute, but many potential witnesses remained. Minority counsel Morris finished the hearings with a list of twenty-five or thirty uncalled witnesses and a strong belief that a new investigation was required. He attempted without success to get the House Committee on Un-American Activities to undertake a probe.[30] But the times were ripe for a new investigation and Morris was not to be disappointed for long.

THE ELECTIONS OF 1950

Before the IPR was sucked into the whirlwind of a full-scale congressional probe, however, the uneasy mood of the

27. Ibid., p. 484. Tydings did not indicate whether the file contained a summary of all information on Lattimore available to the FBI or whether it was a sampling of items at a particular classification level.

28. U.S., Senate, Committee on Foreign Relations, *Report on the State Department Employee Loyalty Investigation* (Report No. 2108), 81st Cong., 2d sess., 1950, pp. 16-17, 72-73.

29. See *Tydings Hearings*, p. 2517.

30. Morris, *No Wonder We Are Losing*, p. 115.

nation was made more apparent by the Congressional elections of 1950. During the campaign both domestic fears and concerns over foreign policy setbacks were skillfully manipulated by hard-driving challengers. To make matters worse, the issues were dramatized on election eve by highly publicized accounts of the massive Chinese Communist intervention in the Korean War. The specter of American boys being cut down by troops from the new Red regime was powerful new support for those who had cried conspiracy in America's China policy.

James Reston, reviewing the 1950 Congressional election campaign, called it a "triumph of 'McCarthyism.'" Reston noted that many Republican candidates had made the conspiracy theory a common theme of their attacks against the administration's foreign policy. Representative Richard Nixon made "anticommunism" virtually the only issue of his hard-swinging Senate campaign in California against Helen Gahagan Douglas. In Maryland, supporters of a virtually unknown Senate candidate, John Marshall Butler, passed out composite pictures of a smiling Senator Tydings shaking hands with ex-Communist party chief Earl Browder.[31] The results were a stunning show of the political impact of "McCarthyism." Nixon was a comfortable winner; Tydings was defeated and even Senate Majority Leader Scott Lucas, the author of the legislation establishing the Tydings Committee, lost his seat.

THE POLITICAL WINDS AND IPR FINANCES

America's tense new political mood came at a very unfortunate time for the IPR. Since its inception, the institute had been heavily dependent on foundation support, especially from the Rockefeller Foundation.[32] Financial crises were chronic in the institute, but an especially serious situation had developed in 1945 when the Rockefeller Foundation made a major policy decision to shift its support from one single Asian studies organization to a number of newly established university area-studies centers. Such a decision, coming on the heels of the Kohlberg assault, raised immediate questions about the viability of the institute.

31. *New York Times*, October 31, 1950.
32. *McCarran Hearings*, pp. 4850-51.

After a period of negotiations, it was finally decided that the Rockefeller Foundation would grant the IPR a five-year terminal grant. During this period, it was hoped that the institute would find new sources of revenue to replace the gradually decreasing Rockefeller grant.[33]

Both the continuing Kohlberg attack and the emergence of Cold War attitudes in the United States made this a very difficult task. By the beginning of the McCarthy period in 1950, no new support had been found. The institute turned again to the Rockefeller Foundation, hoping to gain a short extension. IPR officials at first were concerned that publicity about Frederick Field's support of Communist activities would hinder their application for funds. William Holland wrote Owen Lattimore in mid-September to say that a *Saturday Evening Post* article on Field had "thrown the Rockefeller people into another dither."[34] Shortly thereafter, however, it was agreed that Rockefeller would extend an additional two-year terminal grant of sixty thousand dollars to the IPR and twenty-five thousand dollars to the AIPR.[35] Thus, as the McCarthy period came into full bloom, the institute was barely keeping its head above the financial waters.

"McCARTHYISM" IN PERSPECTIVE

As our analysis earlier in this chapter has suggested, it would be wrong to look at "McCarthyism" mainly in terms of machinations of one senator, no matter how devoted he was to capitalizing on the fears of the times. It would be even less valid to link "McCarthyism" with an account of the "China Lobby" as an explanation for the increasing rigidity in America's Asian policy or internal politics during the early 1950's. Many factors were responsible, some of them having nothing to do with McCarthy or American supporters of Chiang. It is especially important to recognize that "McCarthyism" was a peculiarly American phenomenon. No other Western democracy experienced it during the 1950's, although other states had to react to many of the same developments on the international scene. Although in an objective sense

33. Davis, "The Dissolution of the IPR," p. 127.
34. Holland to Lattimore, September 13, 1950, Columbia Files.
35. Davis, "The Dissolution of the IPR." p. 127.

Australia's security was surely more affected than that of the United States by events on the China mainland, Australians did not react with such apparent passion to the "loss of China." The British public, although it had a significant economic stake in China, did not engage in large scale post-mortems about why British policy had failed to prevent Communist victory. Instead, Britain recognized Peking in the hope—unsuccessful, as events were to show—that some of its business interests in China could be salvaged.

These comparisons suggest that more than historical factors need to be noted in understanding "McCarthyism" in America. The next chapter will examine how senators far less publicity seeking and more durable than McCarthy refined his campaign and in the process dealt a strong blow to the future of the IPR.

4

The McCarran Committee and the IPR

FOR a fleeting moment after the release of the Tydings Committee report, it seemed that the IPR might escape the full force of America's emotional and ugly new mood on the Far East. Even the entry of Chinese forces into the Korean War and the rough-and-tumble congressional elections of 1950 had not resulted in public demands that the institute be investigated. When it happened, it was not only the result of the tenacity of its foes, but also a stroke of fate.

For several years, largely as an economy measure, the old files of the IPR had been stored in a barn on Edward Carter's farm at Lee, Massachusetts. Hearing of their existence, Don Surine, an investigator for Senator McCarthy, reportedly decided to take a look for himself.[1] Without going through the legal niceties of obtaining a search warrant, Surine removed a number of documents from the files and made them available to McCarthy.

McCarthy approached Senator Pat McCarran of Nevada, chief of the Senate Judiciary Committee and also of its newly established Internal Security Subcommittee. McCarran was apparently very interested in what he saw, and the subcommittee secured a subpoena to sequester the IPR files. The files at Lee were seized on February 8, 1951.

---

1. This narrative of the seizure of the files is based on an account provided by Edward Carter from press sources (see *McCarran Hearings*, p. 5353).

From the beginning it was apparent that the McCarran Committee's investigation of the IPR would be far more comprehensive than that of Tydings Committee. It was equally obvious that the new committee would be far less hospitable to institute views. Senator McCarran, the chairman, was well known as a critic of the administration's China policy. In 1949 he had introduced a bill into Congress to provide $1.5 billion in loans to Nationalist China, with the provision that American officers were to direct Chinese troops in the field.[2] McCarran also had the reputation of being a lone wolf secure in his Senate position and an old-fashioned Western conservative with no inclination at all to compromise with the national Democrats.[3]

The other six senators on the Internal Security Subcommittee were balanced by party but not by political philosophy. They were Democrats James Eastland of Mississippi, Herbert O'Conor of Maryland, and Willis Smith of North Carolina, and Republicans Homer Ferguson of Michigan, William Jenner of Indiana, and Arthur Watkins of Utah. All could be classified as conservatives; Jenner had been especially outspoken in his opposition to American policy in China.

In terms of personality and tactics, there were differences among the committee members. For example, Senator O'Conor was never noted for the irascibility or pomposity sometimes displayed by Senator McCarran. Nevertheless, there were many similarities in background and outlook. None of the members could be termed representatives of urban, industrialized America.[4] All could be considered opponents of at least significant portions of the New Deal.

Several of the committee members were highly uneasy about America's national political leadership and were concerned about a seeming loss of national principles. Senator O'Conor believed that some New Dealers and Fair Dealers had been "notoriously cavalier where the security of the United States was at issue."[5] He was especially dismayed at

2. Westerfield, *Foreign Policy and Party Politics*, p. 347.

3. See Alfred Steinberg, "McCarran, Lone Wolf of the Senate," *Harper's Magazine*, 201 (November 1950): 89-95.

4. Although Senator Ferguson represented an urbanized, industrial state, his main bases of support were not in industrial or urban areas.

5. Harry W. Kirwin, *The Inevitable Success: Herbert R. O'Conor*

the Truman administration's attitude toward internal subversion. Senator Ferguson probably spoke for the other
committee members when he declared, "What we need is a
resurgent zeal for America." Such zeal, he believed, had been
"consciously obscured by many sinister influences in this
country in recent decades."[6] Ferguson did not spell out what
"sinister forces" he had in mind.

The composition of the committee staff also gave strong
indication that the IPR was in for some rough sledding.
Robert Morris, the minority counsel at the Tydings hearings,
was chosen special counsel for the IPR investigation to serve
under the direction of Judiciary Committee counsel Jay
Sourwine. Ex-Communist Benjamin Mandel, formerly research director of the House Committee on Un-American
Activities, became chief of research for the McCarran
Committee. No one on the committee staff could have been
termed a specialist on East Asia.

THE HEARINGS

Five months after the seizure of the files, the McCarran
Committee hearings began in Washington.[7] Specifically, the
committee sought to discover:

(a) Whether or to what extent the IPR was infiltrated and
influenced or controlled by agents of the communist world
conspiracy

(b) Whether or to what extent these agents and their dupes
worked throught the Institute into the United States Government
to the point where they exerted an influence on United States far
eastern policy and if so, whether and to what extent they still exert
such influence

(c) Whether or to what extent these agents and their dupes led or
misled American public opinion, particularly with respect to far
eastern policy.[8]

In his opening remarks Senator McCarran asserted the

(Westminster, Md.: Newman Press, 1962), p. 433.

6. *Vital Speeches*, 17 (April 15, 1951): 399.

7. For purposes of emphasis, this chapter will examine actions by
the committee, the content of the hearings and report, and the public
response. The IPR's defense will be included in Chapter 5.

8. U.S., Congress, Senate, Committee on the Judiciary, *Report on the
Institute of Pacific Relations* (Report No. 2050), 82d Cong., 2d sess.,
1952, p. 2 (hereafter cited as *McCarran Report*).

committee's desire for "facts" rather than opinions. The committee members, all lawyers, decided that although their proceedings did not constitute a trial, they would attempt to apply courtroom standards whenever possible.[9] It was also agreed that the proceedings would not be televised and that no photographers would be allowed in the committee room —perhaps in an effort to avoid the klieg-lighted sensationalism of previous sessions of the House Committee on Un-American Activities.

As a general practice, witnesses were examined first in executive session; later, they were given open hearings. This technique was defended by the committee on the grounds that innocent people could be protected from unsubstantiated allegations.[10] The effect, however, was to give a rehearsed effect to the open sessions, since the questioners often knew what type of reply the witness would make. In addition, it left open the possibility that the committee counsel might avoid questions which could lead to answers refuting his preconceptions. It seems very likely that this in fact occurred.

The public hearings began in July 1951 and were completed almost a year later. Edward Carter, former IPR secretary-general, was the first witness. Frederick Field testified next, followed by a series of ex-Communists and professors critical of the IPR. Not until October 10—more than three months after the start of the hearings—did the committee question a current officer of the IPR.

The committee's questioning of the first witness, Edward Carter, gave a good indication of the problems in store for the IPR.[11] Carter was allowed a few moments to provide some background on the institute; then the questioning shifted to

9. See *McCarran Hearings*, p. 519-20.

10. Asked to give a concrete example of this protection, former committee counsel Morris stated that the committee had avoided giving a public session to one witness who had made allegations concerning Mrs. Eleanor Roosevelt (Robert Morris, personal interview, February 8, 1970).

11. It should be noted at this point that any effort to summarize the testimony and exhibits presented before the McCarran Committee is bound to create a misleading impression about the IPR. The unwillingness of the senators and the committee counsel to ask searching questions of the ex-Communists and the professors critical of the IPR,

Frederick Field's role in IPR finances as well as Carter's efforts to secure Field a commission in Army Intelligence in 1942. Carter had barely recovered from these embarrassing lines of inquiry when Counsel Morris read him sections of Owen Lattimore's "cagey" letter of July 10, 1938, and asked him, in effect, to read Lattimore's mind of an earlier decade.

More than seventy at the time of the hearings, Carter was a small shadow of the handsome, supercharged man who had built the IPR into the pre-eminent Asian studies organization. Perplexed, often contrite, his memory sometimes failing, he did not present a good image of the IPR. His contributions were quickly passed over; his shortcomings were explored at length and easily distorted by members of the committee to suggest an affinity for communism on the part of the IPR. A good example of this process was provided by Senator Eastland's interrogation of Carter with regard to the "cagey" letter.

SENATOR EASTLAND:	What did he mean by "cagey?"
MR. CARTER:	Did I use the word?
SENATOR EASTLAND:	No; he said that in his letter. What did he mean by "cagey"; that you were cagey to turn it over to some Communists? That is what they were.
MR. CARTER:	He was attributing a skill or motive that I did not implement and carry out. I think he probably was trying to pay me a compliment.
SENATOR EASTLAND:	Pay you a compliment to turn over that China section there to Communists, noted Communists?[12]

That the committee intended to use documentary material from the IPR files to test the veracity of a witness rather than to help his memory was also demonstrated very quickly during the interrogations of Carter. Asked about his efforts to get Field an Army commission, Carter requested that Morris provide him with the dates when Field began to write

coupled with the failure of the committee to obtain expert opinion about the content of IPR publications, virtually assured such a result. Even when the exhibits presented by the IPR are included, a balanced picture cannot be obtained, since the institute had no opportunity to question directly witnesses making allegations against the IPR.

12. *McCarran Hearings*, p. 37

for the *New Masses* and the *Daily Worker*. Morris made no effort to refresh Carter's memory, despite the fact that such material was available in the IPR files held by the committee.[13]

During his testimony, Carter conceded that in 1942 he had attempted to assist Field in obtaining a commission in Army Intelligence, despite misgivings over Field's connection with the American Peace Mobilization. Carter admitted that his efforts looked "a little fishy now." At the time, however, he had believed that Field would be helpful to the war effort and loyal to the country.[14]

Lattimore's famous "cagey" letter was the foundation of many committee questions to Edward Carter. As the following sequence illustrates, he was pressed very hard to explain how Lattimore had obtained the impression that Carter had "turned over" the China section of the Inquiry to Asiaticus, Ch'en Han-seng, and Chi Ch'ao-ting.

THE CHAIRMAN:	Where did he get the information?
MR. CARTER:	You will have to ask him. I don't know. I know the information was wrong.
THE CHAIRMAN:	He did not get it from you?
MR. CARTER:	Well as I send out—
THE CHAIRMAN:	Answer my question. He did not get that information from you? . . .[15]

Carter stated that he had not accepted Lattimore's advice, with regard to either the Inquiry Series or the position which the institute should take on the policies of various countries, including China and the USSR.

Despite the fact that the committee had in its possession Carter's reply to the "cagey" letter, it was not introduced as evidence during Carter's testimony.[16] However, evidence was offered showing that Chi Ch'ao-ting had been employed on the Inquiry Series, although he had not completed his work. Additional exhibits offered by Counsel Morris showed that (1) Asiaticus had written for Communist publications as

13. Ibid., pp. 17-19, 967. The information about Field's association with the *New Masses* and the *Daily Worker* is available in the *McCarran Report*, p. 143.

14. *McCarran Hearings*, pp. 11, 23.

15. Ibid., pp. 59, 60.

16. Ibid., p. 63.

early as 1927; (2) Carter had been very friendly with Soviet officials, even during the Hitler-Stalin Pact; and (3) in 1938 Carter had suggested to a Canadian organization that United States Communist party chief Earl Browder might be an interesting speaker.[17]

After the hearings were completed, Carter sent the committee a long statement attempting to clarify some of the questions which had been put to IPR witnesses. In answer to questions why the AIPR leadership had not ordered an outside investigation of the Kohlberg charges, Carter asserted that the Executive Committee did not require such an inquiry, since it knew that the institute was not a front for communism. He also denied that he knew Ch'en Han-seng, Chi Ch'ao-ting, and Asiaticus as Communists while they were writing for the IPR. On the issue of his promotion of the Israel Epstein's *Unfinished Revolution in China*, Carter noted that it was not an IPR publication. He thought that it contained useful material and that experienced people such as Senator Arthur Vandenburg and Secretary of State George Marshall would not be "thrown off balance" by it. Finally, he stated that the institute had deliberately refused to take only "safe" issues and had welcomed controversy. It had no choice but to show "unpalatable" as well as "palatable" viewpoints.[18]

The main case for the IPR was presented by Secretary-General William Holland. Prior to his testimony on October 9, 1951, Holland submitted a long statement defending the institute. Holland was not allowed to read his statement, but it was included in the written record. Holland emphasized the nonpartisan nature of the IPR and denied that it was either controlled by Communists or engaged in an effort to influence government policies. To support these arguments, he referred to Soviet statements attacking the IPR as well as former State Department Far Eastern Affairs Division chief Joseph Ballantine's view that he had not seen efforts by the IPR to influence United States policy.[19]

17. Ibid., pp. 48, 151, 175.

18. Ibid., pp. 5341-51.

19. William L. Holland, "Fact and Fiction about the Institute of Pacific Relations," in *McCarran Hearings*, pp. 1212-31. As evidence of Ballantine's views, Holland quoted a portion of a recent letter from the former State Department official.

The committee's unwillingness to assist the IPR in even small matters was demonstrated shortly after Holland's arrival. The committee members first expressed their disapproval of the fact that Holland had told newsmen in advance of his intention to read a statement. Holland then asked Senator Eastland, who was presiding, whether he thought it discourteous to release the statement to reporters. Eastland made no response but simply asked Counsel Morris to begin the questioning.[20]

During his testimony, Holland stated that only in 1945 did he become aware of the use of pseudonyms by IPR staff members Frederick Field and Chi Ch'ao-ting. He also challenged Morris' assertion that Chi was an important IPR personage. Holland conceded that Lawrence Rosinger played some role in the institute, but he defended the objectivity of Rosinger's scholarship in books such as *China's Wartime Politics* and *India and the United States*.[21]

During his second appearance before the committee on March 19, 1952, Holland presented a statement which criticized the committee's apparent failure to appraise a large sample of IPR publications previously provided by the institute. He also urged the committee to subpoena persons who had served in influential policy-making positions and ask them if they had observed any IPR efforts to influence policy. Finally, he noted that no witness had claimed that the IPR was under Communist control as of the time of the hearings.[22]

Frederick Field made a brief appearance at the hearings and surprised no one by invoking his Fifth Amendment privilege on all key questions. After Field came a large number of ex-Communists, all of whom were asked to tell what they knew about Communists in government and the academic and literary fields. Some of the persons named had an important relationship to the IPR; others had little or none. Ex-Communist witnesses received exceedingly polite treatment; they were seldom if ever questioned closely and their testimony was usually accepted at face value.[23]

20. Ibid., pp. 1139-43.
21. Ibid., pp. 1139-71.
22. Ibid., pp. 3891-97.
23. For the treatment of ex-Communist witnesses, see especially

Louis Budenz was again a key witness, as he had been at the Tydings hearings a year earlier. Essentially, Budenz repeated the allegations he had made before the Tydings Committee. This time, however, he testified that party leaders had told him the IPR was not merely penetrated by a Communist cell; it was also a "captive organization, completely under the control of the Communist Party," despite the fact that not all of its personnel may have been under party control. Budenz also referred to the words of Alexander Trachtenburg, a high Communist official. According to Budenz, Trachtenburg had called the IPR "the little red school house for teaching certain people in Washington how to think with the Soviet Union in the Far East." Budenz also listed Lawrence Rosinger, then on the IPR staff, and former staffer Harriet Moore as Communists. Perhaps Budenz' most sensational new charge, however, was that John Fairbank, a Harvard historian, had been termed a Communist by party officials.[24]

Elizabeth Bentley partially corroborated Budenz' testimony, although her evidence, like his, was largely of a hearsay nature. Miss Bentley testified that Golos, her superior in the Communist underground, had told her to avoid the IPR since it was "red as a rose." She described Field as the "political commissar" of the party unit within the IPR and identified Michael Greenberg, a former editor of *Pacific Affairs*, as a member of her underground unit.[25]

An additional feature of the McCarran hearings was the appearance of two former Soviet officials, Alexander Barmine and Igor Bogolepov. Both testified on the question of how the Soviet government had regarded the IPR. Barmine, a former Soviet diplomat and military officer, termed the Institute a "cover shop" for Soviet intelligence. Bogolepov, a former counselor of the Soviet Foreign Office, asserted that the institute was a "two-way track" on which the USSR received military intelligence information about the United States and provided views it wanted the United States government

---

ibid., pp. 412-42, 513-632. The uncritical acceptance of the testimony of the ex-Communists is present throughout the *McCarran Report*, especially pp. 151-59.

24. *McCarran Hearings*, pp. 517, 629.

25. Ibid., pp. 437, 415, 413.

and public to believe. Pressed for some details on this point by Senator Watkins, Bogolepov testified this was his "impression" and said he had not been directly connected with Soviet military intelligence.[26]

Several persons associated with the IPR appeared at the hearings to deny allegations which had been raised against them by previous witnesses. Joseph Barnes, John Fairbank, T. A. Bisson, and Maxwell Stewart all denied that they had been members of the Communist party. In executive session, Bisson denied that his controversial article on "democratic" and "feudal" China had been written on orders from the party.[27] Miriam Farley, an important staff member of the AIPR, disputed claims by Professor David Rowe that he editing of a manuscript about the Huk movement in the Philippines illustrated a pro-Communist bias. In rebutting Rowe's claims, Miss Farley introduced several passages in the final version which identified the Huks as Communists.[28]

Observers with even sketchy knowledge of Owen Lattimore's testimony at the Tydings hearings could have predicted a sharp confrontation between the Johns Hopkins professor and the McCarran Committee. They were not disappointed. Just as he had done a year earlier, Lattimore strode into the committee room with a long, harshly worded statement which on this occasion attacked his accusers and questioned the impartiality of the committee. Lattimore was allowed to read his statement, but before he had finished more than a few lines, he was interrupted by senators insisting that he document his assertions. A series of lengthy verbal skirmishes ensued, which amply demonstrated the mutual hostility between the witness and the committee.[29]

Although Lattimore spent some two weeks on the witness stand, few factual data were developed. Lattimore was pressed for an explanation of parts of the "cagey" letter as well as his rationale for employing writers later described as Communists. His responses obviously did not satisfy any of

26. Ibid., pp. 202, 449.
27. Ibid., p. 5426. Bisson stated that he had not been given an opportunity to repeat his denial during his public testimony.
28. Ibid., p. 4446.
29. See ibid., pp. 2899 and following.

the committee members. Amid all the heat, one rare moment of light may have been provided when Senator O'Conor asked why he had not questioned Field about his reference to "Communist phrases and words" in the draft article by William Brandt for the September 1940 issue of *Pacific Affairs*. Lattimore's response suggests a good deal about the times as well as his own personality: "All I can answer, Senator, is that in the atmosphere of that type, . . . that just wasn't customary in the circles in which I moved."[30]

A surprise for the IPR leadership appeared in the testimony of several East Asian specialists.[31] Professors William Mc-Govern and Kenneth Colegrove of Northwestern University, David Rowe of Yale University, and George Taylor and Karl Wittfogel of the University of Washington all gave derogatory testimony in regard to the objectivity of either the IPR as a whole or a few of its leaders. In one sense, their testimony was a reflection of the deep divisions among Asian specialists which were finally breaking into the open after years of surface calm. But the method in which the divisions were expressed was an indication of the bitterness which had gradually infected the East Asian scholars since the development of the Cold War and the establishment of a Communist China.

Unlike witnesses testifying on behalf of the IPR, the professors critical of the institute were allowed considerable latitude in presenting their views. Rarely were they interrupted or asked for factual data to support their assertions. David Rowe offered his view that Owen Lattimore was a "fellow-traveler" and the "principal [ideological] agent of Stalinism" in the United States.[32] William McGovern stated that Lattimore had always followed the Stalinist line and had tried to advocate it in *Pacific Affairs*.[33] Kenneth Colegrove asserted that "behind the front, the Institute of Pacific Relations was nothing else than a propaganda organization supporting a [Communist] line."[34]

30. Ibid., p. 3253.
31. William L. Holland, personal interview, March 9, 1970.
32. *McCarran Hearings*, p. 3984.
33. Ibid., p. 1013.
34. Ibid., p. 916.

Doubts about the IPR's objectivity were also furnished by Raymond Dennett, a former AIPR secretary. Dennett testified that when he took over the AIPR secretaryship in 1944, he believed the staff had too much power. He expressed "grave doubts" about the objectivity of some staff members and thought they had failed to present "the complete range of critical comment on the Far East that existed at the time." Unlike some of the academic critics, however, he adamantly refused numerous chances to say that this lack of objectivity resulted from communism or procommunism.[35]

Although the testimony of Dennett and the critical professors was embarrassing to the IPR, much more damaging was the refusal of a small number of past and present IPR officials to deny charges made against them. In addition to Frederick Field, former staffers Harriet Moore and Kathleen Barnes and ex-AIPR trustee Len De Caux declined to answer when asked about previous Communist connections. Most damaging of all was the invocation of Fifth Amendment privileges by Lawrence Rosinger, an important staff member still employed at the time of the hearings.

COMMITTEE PRACTICES

Lack of impartiality by members of congressional committees is not unusual.[36] Especially in loyalty-security hearings, the American congressional investigation has not been distinguished by objectivity or fair play.[37] Whether the investigators have been conservatives or liberals, whether the subject was allegedly rapacious merchants or evil sub-

35. Ibid., p. 948. A review of the IPR files suggests that Dennett was not popular with the staff, but there is no indication in written form of Dennett's concern with staff objectivity. It should be noted that Dennett spent a fair portion of his time as secretary combatting Alfred Kohlberg's charges that IPR publications were flavored with a pro-Communist bias. However, one academic critic told the author that Dennett personally believed the IPR had been infiltrated by Communists.

36. See William L. Morrow, *Congressional Committees* (New York: Charles Scribner's Sons, 1969), p. 93. For an expanded analysis of this topic, see Chapter 7, below.

37. Robert K. Carr's study, *The House Committee on Un-American Activities* (Ithaca, N.Y.: Cornell University Press, 1952), pp. 291-92, discloses defects in committee procedures similar to those apparent in the operations of the McCarran Committee.

versives, elected officials have often used the congressional probe to prove a point, rather than merely to develop information pertinent to legislation. From this vantage point it would be unfair to single out the McCarran Committee's investigation of the IPR as a case study in the abuse of congressional authority.

What emerges most strikingly from these hearings, however, is the stark disparity between the committee's claims to fair play and the proceedings themselves. During the first few sessions, Senator McCarran and his colleagues made a special point of noting that the committee wanted facts rather than publicity and intended to conduct the hearings in a fashion as close to courtroom standards as possible. Clearly, committee practices fell far short of the announced goal. In several areas, the committee breached its own standards.[38] The first involved the use of biased or leading questions. Members of the committee often framed their interrogations in a manner which suggested they were looking not for facts but for confirmation of their own views. Senator Eastland was the worst offender in this regard, as the following example suggests:

SENATOR EASTLAND: You have always read what Owen Lattimore wrote?

MR. MCGOVERN: I will not say I have read every word he has written but I have read several of his books.

SENATOR EASTLAND: What kind of a Communist did you think he was?[39]

Later in the hearings, Senator Eastland had this comment for an IPR witness:

SENATOR EASTLAND: I am at a loss to learn why so many Communists were connected with your organization and why action was not taken against them.[40]

38. This is not to suggest that every member was guilty of such breaches. The conduct of Senator O'Conor, for example, was much closer to the announced standards than that of Senators McCarran or Eastland.

39. *McCarran Hearings*, p. 1012.

40. Ibid., p. 1193.

The Judiciary Committee counsel, Jay Sourwine, also participated in leading questioning. At one point, Sourwine's
tactics drew a spirited response from a witness who had been
generally critical of the IPR:

MR. SOURWINE:	That single reading, as a matter of fact, was enough to impress you so that you still remember the impression that this pamphlet distorted the facts for the benefit of the Soviet Union, did it not?
MR. DENNETT:	You are putting words into my mouth which I don't think I put in there. You said "distorted the facts." I am not an expert on the Soviet Far East, on *Land of the Soviet*, therefore I don't know whether the facts are distorted. I would say such facts as I do know have been interpreted most favorably in that, more favorably than I would have done so.[41]

On another occasion, Senator Ferguson indicated he had
made up his mind with regard to the relationship between the
Soviet Council and the policies of the International Secretariat:

SENATOR FERGUSON:	Mr. Lattimore, isn't it true that at the meeting in Moscow in 1936 the party line was established for Pacific Affairs and the Institute and that after that day they [the Soviet Council] remained in and finally did taper off because the party line was being carried on and it could be carried on much better if they didn't appear in the organization? Isn't that a fair conclusion from these documents here today?[42]

A second form of bias was contained in the differing requirements placed upon different witnesses. Critics of the IPR were
generally questioned politely and even deferentially; they
were allowed to place in the record virtually any sort of
opinion without challenge;[43] on the other hand, the committee

41. Ibid., p. 959.
42. Ibid., p. 3251
43. See Herbert L. Packer, *Ex-Communist Witnesses* (Stanford,
Calif.: Stanford University Press, 1962), p. 162.

counsel and members suddenly became extremely "fact-conscious" when questioning those whose views tended to support the IPR. Even when such witnesses presented factual data, they were not necessarily given impartial treatment. A case in point is the questioning of columnist Joseph Alsop. A volunteer witness, Alsop had contradicted Louis Budenz' assertion that Vice-President Henry Wallace's 1944 trip to China had carried out a Communist objective. Although he was hardly an enthusiastic supporter of Lattimore or the IPR and despite the fact that he was presenting a first-hand view of the situation, Alsop was treated very roughly by the committee.[44]

A third committee shortcoming involved periodic interruption of witnesses in the middle of their responses. In some cases, the witness was asked to be responsive to the question, even though he had barely begun. In others, he was required to give a "yes" or "no" answer first before his explanation, even though the question might not be subject to such treatment.[45]

Finally, and most seriously, there is strong evidence that the committee chairman, Senator McCarran, prejudged the case before all the evidence was in. At one point in the hearings, McCarran greeted a witness with the accolade, "Barmine has the courage to come forward with the truth."[46] Moreover, on November 16, 1951, some seven months before the completion of the investigation, he told an interviewer from *U.S. News and World Report:*

I can give you a curbstone opinion from what I have seen of it. The IPR was originally an organization with laudable motives. It was taken over by Communist design and made a vehicle for American policy with regard to the Far East. It was also used for

44. See *McCarran Hearings*, pp. 1403-89. Alsop claimed that the Wallace mission could not be considered favorable to Communist objectives, since its major result was a recommendation to remove General Stilwell from command. Alsop's account seems a good deal more convincing than the one presented by Budenz. The Budenz-Alsop conflict appears to be another situation in which Budenz' information, when capable of an independent check, does not hold up well.

45. See ibid., pp. 3155, 3236-37.

46. Ibid., p. 330.

espionage purposes to collect and channel information of interest or value to the Russian Communists.[47]

THE CHARGES REVEALED

On July 2, 1952, almost a year after the beginning of hearings which produced some five thousand pages of testimony and documents, the McCarran Committee issued its report. Signed by all the members of the Judiciary Committee, the report was a lengthy 226-page document summarizing the attitudes and evidence which led to the committee's conclusions about the IPR. Just as institute officials had feared, the McCarran Committee report was a stinging indictment of the IPR.

The report began by reaffirming the committee's desire for objectivity. Next came a discussion about the difficulty of obtaining evidence when a conspiracy—in this case the Communist party—was involved. Without any dissent from the committee, Senator McCarran asserted that in such cases, very often the only persons able to give evidence would be the conspirators themselves, that is, the ex-Communists. He went on to claim that it was "possible to verify the loyalty of an ex-Communist, in large part, by the very extent of his willingness to give full and frank testimony against the Communist party." The committee members also agreed that when a conspiracy was established or was in the process of being established, hearsay testimony could be received.[48]

An additional preliminary consideration was how to define the word, "Communist." The report acknowledged that definition of this term was difficult, and that IPR representatives had differed from the committee on this point. Noting the wide spectrum of those who participate in the Communist movement, the report asserted that a "broad basis" was necessary to define it; that is, "Communist" was a term "used to connote a person under Communist discipline or who has voluntarily and knowingly cooperated with Communist Party members in furtherance of Communist Party objectives."[49] The report went on to stretch this "broad basis" even further when it declared, "From the standpoint of our

47. *U.S. News and World Report*, 31 (November 16, 1951): 27.
48. *McCarran Hearings*, pp. 5-8.
49. *McCarran Report*, pp. 122-23.

national security it should be noted that a well-intentioned but fuzzy-minded fellow traveler can be almost as dangerous as a knowing conspirator. From the standpoint of Joseph Stalin, he can be equally fruitful merely by serving as an unwitting instrument of Communist trickery."[50]

The conclusions of the committee were numerous and stretched on for several pages. For the purposes of this account it will suffice to summarize the most important and sensational charges raised.[51] These were: (1) the IPR had "not maintained the character of an objective, scholarly, and research organization"; (2) the IPR was controlled by a small core of officials and staff members; "members" of this core were "either Communist or pro-Communist"; (3) the American Communist party and Soviet officials had considered the IPR "as an instrument of Communist policy, propaganda and military intelligence"; (4) "Owen Lattimore was, from some time beginning in the 1930's, a conscious articulate instrument of the Soviet conspiracy"; (5) "Frederick V. Field was no less a Communist at his desk in the IPR office than when he reported to the Politburo of the American Communist Party, or handed in his column to the *Daily Worker*"; (6) "during the period 1945-49, persons associated with the Institute of Pacific Relations were instrumental in keeping United States policy on a course favorable to Communist objectives in China"; (7) "a chief function of the IPR has been to influence United States public opinion"; (8) "the net effect of IPR activities on United States public opinion has been such as to serve international Communist interests and to affect adversely the interests of the United States." The report also recommended that the Department of Justice submit to a grand jury the questions of whether Owen Lattimore or John P. Davies had committed perjury before the committee.[52]

50. Ibid., p. 123.

51. Readers who desire an extensive discussion of the McCarran Committee report are referred to Carpenter, "The Institute of Pacific Relations." In general the author believes that Carpenter's work contains much useful material but is one-sidedly critical of the IPR and is deficient in failing to examine the definitions and general frame of reference employed by the McCarran Committee.

52. *McCarran Report*, pp. 96, 223-26. Davies was a foreign service officer who had specialized in Chinese affairs.

The committee's conclusions were supported and spelled out in much greater detail in the body of the report. For the most part, the report was a summary of the allegations raised against the IPR devoid of any critical analysis. Occasionally, reference was made to claims made by IPR spokesmen, but generally as a means of refuting them.

The extent to which the McCarran Committee had accepted the testimony of the ex-Communist witnesses was evident in a long table entitled, "Summary of Communist Affilations by Individuals with Their IPR Functions." Although a number of the eighty-seven names on the list had been identified as Communists, many had only the most minimal connection with the IPR.[53] In addition, a number of prominent IPR personalities such as William Holland, William Lockwood, and Miriam Farley were listed solely on the grounds that they participated in organizations or had written for press services considered by the committee to be "pro-Communist".[54]

In presenting the report to the Senate, Senator McCarran asserted that he was "convinced, from the evidence developed in this inquiry, that, but for the machinations of the small group that controlled and activated that organization, China today would be free and a bulwark against the further advance of the Red hordes into the Far East".[55] While the committee report does not contain such an expansive conclusion, it is quite possible that the committee members shared Senator McCarran's belief. At any rate, none came forward to dispute their chairman's view.

In addition to problems of definition and methodology, there are a host of rejoinders and reservations which could be raised to the conclusions of the McCarran Committee. Only a few will be discussed here. First, it should be noted that, despite its disparaging remarks about the institute, the McCarran Committee did not conduct an inquiry to determine whether or not the IPR was an objective research

53. For example, Frank Coe was listed because he had attended one IPR conference. See ibid., p. 152. Coe worked for the Treasury Department during World War II.

54. Ibid., pp. 153-55.

55. *Congressional Record*, 98 (July 2, 1952): 8859.

organization. Its task was to determine whether Communists had infiltrated the IPR and whether the institute had influenced foreign policy or public opinion. In the process the committee at times came across data which reflected—sometimes adversely—on IPR objectivity. The evidence was hardly definitive, however. Had objectivity been a major question, fairness would have required the McCarran Committee both to take the testimony of neutral scholars and to obtain expert opinion on the nature of the total IPR product. These tasks were not performed.

In fact, it can easily be concluded that the IPR *per se* was not of much importance to Senator McCarran and his associates. Thus, the committee report failed to give the reader any notion of the West Coast resistance to Edward Carter's leadership or the movement to remove Frederick Field from a position of executive responsibility in the IPR. Still less did the committee make it clear that relatively few of the individuals it had listed as "Communists" or "pro-Communists" held important positions in the institute at the time of the hearings. Neither did the report make much effort to show that officials such as Frederick Field were Communists at the time they were actively participating in IPR affairs. In fact, a time frame is often missing from the report, especially when its use might detract from the conclusions of the committee. Had the committee possessed real interest in the future of an Institute of Pacific Relations, it surely could have made some effort to distinguish between past and present problems and to credit the IPR in the areas of its success. The committee's failure in this respect again suggests that, more than anything else, it considered the IPR investigation as an instrument for influencing America's foreign and domestic policy.

It is precisely in the area of foreign policy that the conclusions of the McCarran Committee are the most tenuous. Had it desired to do so, the committee no doubt could have made a substantial case that Edward Carter at times used his IPR position in an effort to influence American foreign policy toward China. In addition, it could have provided evidence that Laurence Salisbury edited *Far Eastern Survey* in such a fashion as to suggest he was hoping to influence that policy. Instead, the committee chose to conclude with the vague but sweeping assertion that persons "associated" with the IPR were instrumental in keeping United States China policy on a path "favorable" to Communist objectives in China. No witnesses familiar with the development of United States policy presented evidence to support this assertion;[56] neither did the committee explain how such a change was sold to the prime movers of United States policy at the time, President Harry S. Truman and Secretary of State Dean Acheson.

A striking feature of the report was its failure to give the reader any notion of the many forces which influence American opinion and foreign policy. Instead, the reader was left with the impression that one small and poorly financed organization—in this case, the IPR—could have a decisive influence on both. Why senators long familiar with both executive and congressional powers in foreign policy should leave such an impression is one of the unanswered questions of the McCarran hearings.

THE PUBLIC'S VIEW

Before assessing the immediate significance of the McCarran Committee hearings and report on the IPR, it is worthwhile to present a rough reconstruction of these events as they appeared in the public press. Probably very few Americans bothered to read the committee's 226-page report. Even fewer likely perused the massive record of the hearings. Thus, the public's viewpoint was heavily dependent on the account it received in the press and popular journals.

56. The one witness with direct knowledge of American China policy was Stanley Hornbeck, former chief of the State Department's Division of Far Eastern Affairs. Hornbeck testified that in 1945 there had been a change in United States policy which he had opposed. However, Hornbeck did not suggest that the change occurred as a result of pressure from persons "associated" with the IPR. See *McCarran Hearings*, p. 5363. After the hearings, Hornbeck told reporter Don Oberdorfer that he had seen no special IPR effort to influence U.S. policy. Hornbeck was critical of both Lattimore and the IPR, but believed the latter's influence on policy was "practically none." See Oberdorfer, "The McCarran Committee's Investigation," p. 92.

Daily newspapers provided one source of public information.[57] Few papers were able to send their own reporters to the hearings; most relied on reports from the Associated Press or the *New York Times*. Generally speaking, the daily press focused its coverage not on the IPR but on the more controversial confrontation between the McCarran Committee and Owen Lattimore. Most journals summarized the allegations made against various IPR officials; less frequently, they carried the rebuttals of institute spokesmen. Editorial comment during the hearings was sparse; in the *New York Times*, columnist Arthur Krock criticized the conduct of the hearings, saying they were unbalanced and failed to give accused individuals an adequate opportunity to defend themselves.[58] William S. White, who had covered many congressional investigations for the *Times*, may have had similar misgivings. Writing in early 1952, White did not single out the McCarran Committee, but merely noted the tendency of congressional investigations to become "punitive rather than fact-finding."[59]

Perhaps because it was released during the stormy 1952 Republican convention, the McCarran Committee report did not receive major play in the daily press. Most papers summarized the committee's conclusions but again stressed the confrontation between the senators and Owen Lattimore, this time in the form of the committee's contention that Lattimore had provided false testimony. In the sample examined, only four papers commented editorially on the committee report. The *Washington Post*, which had been skeptical of the McCarran Committee from the beginning, termed the report "an attempt to perpetrate another fraud and hoax on the American people."[60] The *Chicago Tribune*, whose coverage had been consistently favorable to the committee during the hearings, predictably endorsed the committee findings.

57. This analysis is based on a survey of the following papers: *Atlanta Constitution, Chicago Tribune, Christian Science Monitor, Los Angeles Times, New York Herald-Tribune, New York Times, San Francisco Chronicle, Seattle Post-Intelligencer*, and the *Washington Post*.

58. *New York Times*, October 11, 1951.

59. William S. White, "An Inquiry into Congressional Inquiries," *New York Times Magazine*, March 23, 1952, p. 25.

60. *Washington Post*, July 4, 1952.

The *Los Angeles Times*, seemingly impressed by the evidence cited in the committee report, termed it a "thoroughly considered document" and expressed its approval of the committee's conclusions regarding Lattimore.[61] This last attitude suggests that the heavy documentation and skillful editing of the McCarran report made it a far more convincing document to the nonspecialist than Alfred Kohlberg's rambling charges of a few years earlier.

Perhaps the most balanced press coverage of the report was provided by the *New York Herald-Tribune*. On the one hand, it ran a column by David Lawrence giving a sympathetic view of the committee's conclusions. In its own editorial, the *Herald-Tribune* told its readers that the committee had presented some evidence showing that some IPR personnel had deviated from their role as objective researchers. However, it found Senator McCarran's statement linking the IPR to the "loss of China" a "curious oversimplification".[62]

In view of the relatively sparse press coverage given to the McCarran hearings and report, it is a fair guess that most Americans gained a viewpoint on the IPR mainly through accounts in mass-circulation journals. On the whole, it was an image highly unfavorable to the IPR. Both *Time* and *Newweek* covered the hearings and report without raising questions or criticism about committee procedures or standards of evaluation. *Time* especially left no doubt that it accepted the committee's conclusions. The *Saturday Evening Post* was convinced from a review of the testimony that the institute had been "heavily infiltrated by Communists and fellow travelers."[63]

Readers of smaller-circulation journals received quite a different view. As one might expect, the *Nation*, a liberal journal, was sharply critical of the conduct of the hearings. Probably the most balanced account of the hearings was provided by *Commonweal*, a Catholic publication. In an action not followed by their competitors, *Commonweal*'s

61. *Chicago Tribune*, July 6, 1952; the *Los Angeles Times*, July 5, 1952.

62. *New York Herald-Tribune*, July 4, 1952.

63. *Time*, 60 (July 14, 1952): 25-26; "Some Odd Problems Used to Worry the Institute of Pacific Relations," *Saturday Evening Post*, 24 (January 19, 1952): 12.

editors chose an author familiar with Asian problems, Harold Hinton. An Asian specialist not closely connected to the IPR, Hinton was able to bring to his analysis a perspective often missing from reporting about the IPR case. Hinton presented a mixed picture about the IPR. On the one hand, he believed that "many" institute publications had "reflected an arid leftist outlook." However, Hinton attributed this condition not to any sinister design but to the immaturity of Far Eastern scholarship from a generation of intellectuals who had come of age during the Depression. He also argued that the IPR was only one force among many which influenced America's Far Eastern policy.[64]

As can be surmised from the above survey, an unusually diligent reader might have been able to obtain sufficient data to allow him to make some tentative judgments about the IPR. The average reader, however, was given very little perspective. For the most part, he was bombarded with a series of charges and countercharges and occasional angry denials. Although probably somewhat bewildered by the whole controversy, he was likely left with the vague feeling that there was some connection between Communists and the IPR and that these connections had not been severed.

It is unlikely that the soiling of the IPR's public image was a conscious goal of the McCarran Committee. As we have noted, the nature of the committee hearings and report suggests that the Internal Security Subcommittee members were much more interested in the IPR case as a means of influencing America's foreign and domestic policies. In particular, they likely hoped that the IPR investigation would assist in blocking liberal or leftist influence in government at home and would create an atmosphere favorable to a hard-line anti-Communist policy abroad. In the process, however, they created some severe problems for an organization which already was in serious financial trouble. How the IPR responded to that challenge will be examined next.

64. Harold C. Hinton, "The Spotlight on Pacific Affairs," *Commonweal*, 56 (April 25, 1952): 65-66.

5

The IPR: Struggles against Oblivion

THE RESPONSE

No doubt there were factors in the organization and leadership of the Institute of Pacific Relations which made it unique. Nevertheless, many of the problems faced by the IPR during the McCarran Committee investigation illustrate the types of difficulties which any private scholarly or research organization might encounter with the Congress and American public opinion, especially during periods of protracted Cold War tensions. For this reason, it seems worthwhile to analyze the IPR's strategy in responding to the McCarran Committee, as well as its subsequent efforts to maintain its existence in the face of adverse publicity.

Paradoxically, just as the highlights of past IPR controversies were being spread over the nation's newspapers, the practices of the institute itself were probably less contentious than at any time since Edward Carter assumed effective leadership of the IPR in 1929. By the time of the McCarran hearings, Carter had retired from active leadership, maintaining only his position on the AIPR Executive Committee. His replacement as secretary-general, William Holland, lacked Carter's flamboyance either as an administrator or in his activities outside of the IPR. With one exception, Lawrence Rosinger, the staff members had created little controversy.

For a variety of reasons, institute publications just before and during the hearings exhibited few of the weaknesses which at times had marred IPR scholarship during the 1930's and 1940's. In part, the changes were a result of personality. As noted previously, Philip Lilienthal, who edited *Pacific Affairs* throughout the McCarran hearings, possessed none of Owen Lattimore's strong desire to make that journal a focus of intellectual controversy. In a similar fashion, *Far Eastern Survey* editor Miriam Farley demonstrated none of Laurence Salisbury's desire to editorialize on matters of East Asian politics.

Personality was only one factor. More fundamentally, both journals had begun to feel the full effects of the postwar blooming of Western scholarship on East Asia. No longer was it necessary on occasion for IPR editors to rely on essentially journalistic accounts from writers without adequate background in their fields and sometimes of questionable objectivity. Most often, an undisputed specialist was now available for the job. Names such as James Allen, Abraham Chapman, or "Asiaticus" no longer graced the pages of IPR journals. In their place were well-known academic figures such as Milton Sacks, Robert North, and George Kahin. Especially in their coverage of Chinese politics and America's role in Asia, such writers gave readers of *Pacific Affairs* and *Far Eastern Survey* far more detail and balance than that which had characterized those journals in earlier decades.

Difficulties of Response

Despite the fact that the IPR's leadership and scholarship of 1951 was much less open to criticism than in earlier periods, the institute was faced with a very difficult task in defending itself against the charges raised in the McCarran hearings and report. In the first place, it was not structured for such activity. Of necessity its defense had to be performed by a very small staff already heavily burdened by its regular duties. Its officers and staff were not skilled in public relations; neither did funds exist to hire persons who had such experience.

A second problem was common to all individuals or groups who faced charges of communism during the 1950's. Only rarely would a denial get publicity comparable to the initial charges. Even when it did, the effect was sometimes double-edged, since coverage of rebuttals often gave new publicity to the charges. In the case of the IPR, defense against specific accusations was especially difficult, since the institute's files had been seized by the committee and access was originally denied to IPR officials.[1]

Third, it was not easy to decide what form of defense would be most effective with the McCarran Committee. As the hearings began, it was evident that the IPR would face a generally hostile group of senators; it was not clear, however, whether an effort to avoid public criticism of the committee would bring any benefits.

All of these problems were compounded by an additional factor: dissension in the IPR. Although the Seattle and San Francisco chapters were defunct and most members had greater confidence in the new IPR leadership, there were nevertheless doubts about how the institute should conduct its defense. Some West Coast personalities, who remained as members despite the dissolution of their local chapters, believed that the institute should welcome congressional assistance in uncovering Communist activity in the IPR.[2] Others believed that the new leadership should dissociate itself from certain past actions, especially by Edward Carter and Owen Lattimore. However, the majority of IPR leaders believed that such a defense would only aid the institute's detractors.[3]

The Executive Committee of the AIPR was responsible for coordination of the IPR's response to the McCarran Committee. The membership of the Executive Committee varied somewhat during the hearings, but several individuals were prominent—Gerard Swope, Holland, Lincoln C. Brownell, Sidney Gamble, and L. Carrington Goodrich. Swope, chairman of the AIPR, was an important spokesman during and after the hearings. Day-to-day defense efforts were led by William Holland, International IPR secretary-general and concurrently executive vice-chairman of the AIPR. The

1. Access to the files was finally permitted in March 1952, when IPR officials were given one month to examine them.

2. George Taylor to Gerard Swope, January 22, 1952, Columbia Files.

3. William L. Holland, personal interview, March 18, 1950; Holland to Dr. Kurt Bloch, May 6, 1952, Columbia Files.

assignment would not have been easy for anyone, but Holland was in a particularly difficult position. Although he was not personally vulnerable to the sorts of criticism and charges which had been directed against previous IPR officials such as Carter and Lattimore, he had spent much of his adult life harmoniously working with them. It probably would have been difficult, if not impossible, for him to lead a defense which was openly critical of the previous leadership. In addition, since Edward Carter was still sitting on the AIPR Board of Trustees, it would have been a most unpleasant task for the Executive Committee to authorize such a defense.

Defense of the IPR

Although no definitive decision was made all at once, the institute's strategy of defense evolved as follows: (1) it would admit that all of its officials were fallible, but would not make specific public criticisms of individual policies or leaders;[4] (2) it would at the beginning criticize individual committee actions which it felt unfair but would avoid sweeping statements against the committee; (3) it would make a strong effort to publicize the institute's accomplishments. It should be recalled at this point that the IPR was not a monolithic organization. It had no authority to control the testimony of its own members, nor is there evidence that it attempted to do so. There was always the risk, however, that in the public mind, the testimony of individuals such as Owen Lattimore and Frederick Field would be seen as part of the IPR's defense.

The IPR leadership's first public comment on the McCarran investigation occurred shortly after the seizure of the files. William Holland termed the seizure "unnecessary and melo-dramatic" and added that the committee could have had the files for the asking. He assured reporters that the IPR would cooperate with the committee.[5] Holland then moved to re-assure IPR members about the purposes of the institute. In a letter to subscribers of *Far Eastern Survey*, Holland stated

4. Holland wrote one prominent member to say that criticism of Carter should be kept within the IPR circle in order to maintain confidence in the leadership (Holland to Melvin Conant, October 16, 1952, Columbia Files).

5. *New York Times*, February 12, 1951.

that the IPR had not lobbied or advocated policies; it remained, he said, a nonpartisan scholarly organization.[6]

The IPR's campaign to combat damage to its public image began with the issuance of a short pamphlet describing the purposes and work of the institute.[7] At the same time, work was going forward to secure testimonials on the work of the IPR from leading Asian scholars. A number of the responses were published in pamphlet form in 1951.[8] Of those asked for testimonials, by far the large majority responded in a favorable manner. Perhaps typical was the comment of Eugene Staley, former secretary of the San Francisco IPR and a man who had not always seen eye-to-eye with Edward Carter. Staley believed that "no fair-minded person can inspect the many shelves of substantial, scholarly, and path-breaking studies issued by the IPR . . . and still give belief to the charges that the IPR has been a conspiracy to put over a particular point of view, or that it has been under the domination of Communists."[9]

Not all Asian specialists took such a favorable attitude about the IPR. Kurt Bloch, a former staff member, wrote Holland to complain about what he considered poor editing of the *Far Eastern Survey*.[10] A West Coast scholar strongly criticized Lattimore for his remarks in the "cagey" letter as well as for his comments on the Soviet purge trials controversy. He was also critical of Bisson's article on "democratic" and "feudal" China as well as Harriet Moore's uncritical use of Soviet sources.[11]

Several months after the hearings began, the Executive Committee came to the belief that it had to do more than just present the institute's achievements. The testimony of the ex-Communists was presenting a very negative picture of the IPR and Edward Carter's appearance had done little to alter

6. See Edna McGlynn, "The Institute of Pacific Relations" (Ph.D. diss., Georgetown University, 1959), p. 100.

7. AIPR, *Understanding Asia: The Aims and Work of the Institute of Pacific Relations* (New York, 1951).

8. AIPR, *Testimonials in Support of the Institute of Pacific Relations* (New York, 1951).

9. Staley to Holland, May 4, 1952, Columbia Files.

10. Bloch to Holland, April 20, 1952, Columbia Files.

11. Robert North to Holland, July 3, 1951, Columbia Files.

that impression. Thus, it was decided that the IPR would have to do something to counteract such an image. The new policy involved a calculated risk, since it sometimes included open criticism of committee practices—a tactic unlikely to endear the institute to a group not basically disposed to give great credence to the arguments of IPR leaders.

The IPR's counterattack began on October 9, 1951, with a press release by Gerard Swope, chairman of the AIPR. Swope charged that the McCarran Committee had been presenting an "incomplete and prejudiced" picture of the IPR. He also asked that the institute be given access to its own files.[12] At the same time, William Holland was making an effort to neutralize the unfavorable publicity resulting from the refusals of several current and former staff members and writers to answer questions about their past relationships to the Communist party. During the hearings Holland wrote to each such individual asking for written denials of the charges made against them.[13] The results were not especially helpful to the IPR. None of the persons invoking the Fifth Amendment was willing to make such a denial. Lawrence Rosinger, Harriet Moore, and Kathleen Barnes all told Holland that they feared perjury trials if they were to make such denials, since witnesses at the hearings had already indicated a willingness to testify against them under oath. The most that they were willing to say was that they had seen no evidence of a Communist cell or indications of a line in institute publications during the years in which they were employed by the IPR.[14]

As far as can be determined from the written record, the decision of institute leaders to avoid specific public criticism of past IPR officials was not strongly challenged by the membership. However, the issue was focused for public attention late in 1951 by a nonmember Asian specialist, Richard Walker. In early November, Walker wrote the *New York Times* to complain that the IPR was following an "all-or-nothing" defense of past policies. Since Walker be-

12. *New York Times*, October 10, 1951.
13. William L. Holland, personal interview, March 18, 1970.
14. See Kathleen Barnes to Holland, March 6, 1952, and Harriet Moore to Holland, March 7, 1952, Columbia Files.

lieved that some IPR officials had failed to stay within accepted bounds of scholarly inquiry, he felt that all-out support for
such officials was not the institute's best defense. Holland
replied the next week by denying that the IPR was conducting an "all-or-nothing" defense. He complained that
Walker seemed to want the institute to confess to a multitude
of sins.[15]

The matter rested there for some time, but as the hearings
were nearing completion, the debate over the IPR's defense
strategy was revived as a result of a long article by Walker
in the *New Leader*, a journal of opinion in New York. Walker
was neither totally favorable to the McCarran Committee
nor entirely negative about the achievements of the IPR;
nevertheless, he was highly critical of Lattimore's role in
the institute and termed some of his actions "pro-Communist."
Although Walker conceded that "no treason" was involved
and that Lattimore "had a perfect right" to his views, he
strongly criticized what he believed was bias in Lattimore's
editing of *Pacific Affairs*. Walker believed that Communists
had successfully infiltrated the IPR, but he thought that
the major issue for the institute was objectivity, not communism. In defending itself, he argued, the IPR should not
defend those who had violated its own principles.[16]

In many cases the hard-pressed IPR leadership did not
have adequate time to answer allegations about the institute
raised in the press and popular journals. Perhaps because
Walker was known as an Asian specialist and he had written
a detailed article, however, William Holland was quick to
reply. Without openly defending Lattimore, Holland wrote
the *New Leader* to complain that Walker had failed to
mention Lattimore's explanations of his conduct. He also
denied that Walker's knowledge of the institute was
"intimate and extensive," as claimed by the editors.[17]

Apparently, Holland's rebuttal did not put the matter
to rest for all members of the IPR, for he found it necessary

15. *New York Times*, November 5, 13, 1951.
16. Richard L. Walker, "Lattimore and the IPR," *New Leader*, 35
(March 31, 1952): S1-S16.
17. William L. Holland, "Mr. Holland Objects," *New Leader*, 35
(April 21, 1952): 10-11.

to expand his views in private comments. His reply to one inquirer was typical of his position and is worth quoting at length:

The point is, as you well know, that the whole climate of American opinion has changed so drastically in the last few years that actions and opinions, which in earlier years excited little comment and were certainly not considered as near treason, are judged today in a wholly different light, but the important thing to remember is that this re-evaluation of the past applies not just to IPR officers and staff and not even the IPR membership, but rather to a whole generation of American opinion.[18]

The appearance of the McCarran Committee report faced the IPR with new difficulties. Now that the accusations against it had been stamped with the official approval of a Senate committee, potential donors to the IPR would likely be forced to take a second look at their contributions. In an effort to reassure them as well as the membership, on October 1, 1952, the Executive Committee of the AIPR issued a statement which reaffirmed its confidence in the value of the IPR and in its present leadership. Perhaps in an attempt to take the sting out of the McCarran Committee's charges, the statement conceded—without citing names—that some IPR officials in the past had "occasionally showed poor judgment in not sufficiently dissociating their outside activities as private citizens from their duties on a nonpartisan body." The Executive Committee admitted that some former IPR employees could have been Communists but claimed that the institute had never been under Communist control or engaged in subversive activities.[19]

The IPR's full reply to the McCarran Committee report did not appear until early the next year. At that time the institute released a ninety-four-page report detailing its defense and offering sharp criticism of committee practices. It repeated previous denials that the IPR had ever been under Communist control or had attempted to influence United States foreign policy in a particular direction. However, it acknowledged that a few former IPR employees had shown "poor judgment" in their outside activities by failing

18. Holland to William Phillips, June 26, 1952, Columbia Files.
19. AIPR, *Annual Report*, 1952, pp. 13-14.

to show that they were acting as individuals rather than as IPR officers. The differences between the McCarran Committee and the IPR concerning the definition of key terms and the proper use of institute publications were also thoroughly explored, as was the IPR's contention that the committee had failed to make clear the changing standards by which it had evaluated actions by IPR officials during the 1930's and 1940's.[20]

The IPR's Defense in Review

What was the result of the IPR's efforts to defend itself against the charges raised during the McCarran hearings and in the committee report? Although only rough estimates can be made, they are worth pondering, since they suggest the types of problems which small, private groups encounter in a conflict with congressional investigators, especially during periods of Cold War tensions. For purposes of analysis, it is best to examine the response of three separate groups—IPR members, the senators on the McCarran Committee, and the public.

Of these groups, it is safe to say that the only one to respond favorably to the IPR's defense was its own membership. For the vast majority of those who had been closely associated with the institute for many years, the allegations raised before the McCarran Committee did not ring true. For such supporters the IPR's defense was probably convincing and reassuring.

The effect on the members of the McCarran Committee seems to have been quite the opposite. Although it is doubtful that any type of IPR defense short of abject submission would have been favorably received by the committee, it seems likely that aspects of the IPR's defense boomeranged and resulted in even more harsh treatment by the committee than might normally have been the case. The failure of the institute leaders to curb the severity of Owen Lattimore's assault on the committee very probably antagonized the committee, increased its internal cohesion, and assisted

20. AIPR, *Commentary on the McCarran Report on the IPR*, (New York, 1953), pp. 1-4.

those committee members who had demonstrated the strongest hostility to the IPR.

As for the general public, it is unlikely that the IPR's low-cost defense effort had much impact. Outside of the IPR membership and the Senate investigators, probably very few Americans were aware of the details of the IPR's case. Thus, the IPR's defense probably did little to alter the account often conveyed by the press and mass-circulation journals that stressed Owen Lattimore's role in the IPR, his attacks on the committee, and the allegations of the ex-Communists. Given the nature of the press, public attitudes, the McCarran Committee, and the IPR's leadership and finances, such a result is not surprising. Nevertheless, by early 1953 the IPR's public image had been severely damaged. The importance of this occurrence for the future of the institute was quickly demonstrated.

THE IPR FADES OUT

The effort to combat the charges raised before the McCarran Committee temporarily submerged two far more fundamental problems facing the IPR. With the ending of the investigation, these problems required immediate action.

The first problem involved finance. The Rockefeller grant was soon to terminate and no new source of funding had been found. The charges made in the McCarran hearings naturally gave pause to all potential donors to the IPR. Especially for foundations, these concerns were intensified during late 1952 by a congressional inquiry checking into the uses put to foundation grants. Although the House committee which conducted the hearings eventually exonerated the foundations from charges of misconduct,[21] there was enough display of congressional sentiment to make it clear that grants to controversial groups such as the IPR would not be looked upon favorably by elements in Congress. During the hearings, the chairman, representative E. E. Cox of Georgia, charged that Owen Lattimore had obtained large sums of money from the Rockefeller Foundation and that the money had been used for "subversive purposes."[22] Cox did

21. *New York Times*, December 20, 1954.
22. Ibid., November 26, 1952.

not mention the IPR but the implication was obvious.

During the Cox hearings, Rockefeller Foundation head Dean Rusk was questioned closely about his organization's grants to the IPR. Rusk defended the grants, pointing out that the worth of the great bulk of IPR research had not been called into question. He noted, however, that his foundation had been "concerned" about allegations of bias on the part of the institute staff; he told the congressmen that he regarded the chances of additional grants to the IPR as "remote."[23]

A second, and related, problem concerned the type of program which the institute, and especially the AIPR, intended to pursue during a period of change in the Asian studies field. American university centers of Asian studies, aided by foundation grants, were beginning to spring up. In the process they began to assume some of the functions previously performed primarily by the IPR. Clearly, the times called for a reassessment of the institute's role. The problems facing the American Council were succinctly stated by one of its long-time staff members not long after the completion of the McCarran investigation: "Since the war, with the exception of [*Far Eastern Survey*] (which is good), AMCO has had little program. Most IPR work in the United States has been done by the Secretariat. AMCO's difficulty since 1945 has been not so much McCarran as lack of new program and organization. What do we want to salvage from AMCO? There is not much to salvage except FES and potentialities."[24]

The IPR's stock-taking began in September 1952, when the AIPR Executive Committee set up a Planning and Review Committee. Specifically, the committee was charged with the responsibility of recommending to the board whether or not the AIPR's activities or organization should be modified.[25]

Progress on the review committee was agonizingly slow. Whether this resulted in part from inadequate leadership is

23. U.S., Congress, House of Representatives, Select Committee to Investigate Tax-Exempt Foundations and Comparable Organizations, *Hearings on Tax-Exempt Foundations*, 82d Cong., 2d sess., 1952, pp. 521-29.

24. Miriam Farley to Holland, August 9, 1952, Columbia Files.

25. AIPR, *Annual Report*, 1952, p. 14.

unclear. Probably a more fundamental reason for its lack of progress was the reluctance of well-known personalities in the Asian field to offer definitive advice on the future of the IPR. Few wanted to see the end of the IPR unless there was a new organization willing to take over some of its major responsibilities, and they were unsure of finding such an organization. This problem may have convinced some important scholars in the field that it would not be worthwhile to spend a great deal of time struggling with the troubles of the IPR.

In any event, the IPR experienced considerable difficulty in getting its review committee proceedings off the ground. In February 1953, Antonio de Grassi was appointed head of a group to canvass the views of AIPR members and East Asian specialists on the possible reorganization of the AIPR or the need for a new group to carry out IPR functions. But little progress had been made by October, when de Grassi resigned. By that time matters had come to such difficulty that long-range studies seemed superfluous.

A Crisis Reached

The immediate problems were financial. By the latter part of 1953, the AIPR had failed to secure a replacement for the Rockefeller grant. In addition, corporate giving—always a valuable part of the Institute's income—had declined sharply as a result of the unfavorable publicity from the McCarran investigation. Even companies long faithful to the IPR such as Standard-Vacuum had found it necessary to sever their relationship with the institute in the face of stockholder protests.[26]

In late October the Executive Committee met and recommended dissolution of the AIPR by the end of January. It also decided to hold an enlarged meeting later to discuss its recommendation. Matters moved quickly, and by mid-December William Holland announced that *Far Eastern Survey* would be continued by the IPR International Secretariat but that most other AIPR functions would be suspended.

At this point, the Hawaii chapter announced its decision

26. Draft covering letter, undated, 1953, AIPR, Columbia Files. See also Davis, "The Dissolution of the IPR," pp. 333-35.

to change its name to the "Pacific and Asian Affairs Council" —an action which effectively terminated its relationship with the IPR.[27] Thus, by the end of 1953 the AIPR had lost its founding chapter. The loss of Hawaii, together with the previous dissolution of the San Francisco and Seattle chapters, had removed three of the strongest AIPR units. The future of the AIPR seemed bleak. Since the AIPR and American funds had long formed the bedrock of the International IPR, the chances of salvaging the institute seemed slim.

Back from the Brink

Just as it appeared the American IPR would go under, it received a temporary reprieve. In January 1954, Holland was able to report that the trustees and members had contributed over twelve thousand dollars during a three-week period. In view of this development, an enlarged Executive Committee had unanimously voted to drop the plan for dissolution and to continue the AIPR with a limited program.[28]

It should be noted that the ability of the AIPR to avoid dissolution left no assurance that the organization could ultimately survive. Most of the emergency funds had been collected from individuals who had been long-time supporters of the IPR. Obviously, if the institute were again to become financially viable, it would be necessary to attract a much broader base.

The IPR's problems in obtaining new foundation support were compounded in late 1954 by a new House of Representatives investigation into foundation giving. Headed by Representative B. Carroll Reece of Tennessee, the new committee was far more hostile to the foundations than its predecessor. Its report, issued in December, charged that some large foundations were "directly supporting subversion." The report further alleged that such organizations were part of an "international cartel" which was supporting a socialism of "far greater menace than communism."[29] Unlike the

27. Circular letter to the Members of the AIPR, December 18, 1953, Vancouver Files; J. B. Atherton to Morden Murphy, December 18, 1953, Vancouver Files.

28. Holland to the Trustees of the AIPR, January 12, 1954, Columbia Files.

29. *New York Times*, December 20, 1954.

report of the McCarran Committee, the Reece report brought forth a strong dissent from two committee members. Nevertheless, the warning to the foundations was clear—stay away from grants which would give hostile congressmen an opening.

Several other factors hampered the AIPR's efforts to rebuild. In the first place, not everyone was happy with the decision to continue. Not long after the decision was announced, Holland received a protest from a prominent Hawaii member, who saw it as evidence that a small group of people had exerted excessive influence over the IPR.[30]

A second problem involved the need to draw up a program for the AIPR. The Executive Committee decided that it would send a delegate to the International IPR conference scheduled for 1954 in Kyoto. Long-range decisions proved more difficult, however. A new Planning Committee was established in May 1954. It met several times during the next year in an effort to resolve the question of the AIPR's future. When it had finished, however, it could conclude only that, while a stronger Asian studies group was needed, nothing was on the horizon and the AIPR should therefore continue its work.[31]

While the IPR was grappling with its problems, a more personal drama was unfolding, but one of intense interest to the institute. It should be recalled that the McCarran Committee had recommended that the Justice Department consider seeking perjury indictments against John Paton Davies and Owen Lattimore as a result of their testimony before the committee. Insufficient evidence was found to seek a grand jury indictment of Davies,[32] but a case against Lattimore did go forward. On December 16, 1952, a federal grand jury indicted him on seven counts of perjury based upon his testimony before the committee. The counts ranged from charges he had lied when he said he had "never been a sympathizer or any other kind of a promoter of Communist in-

30. Melvin Conant to Holland, January 12, 1954, Vancouver Files.

31. AIPR, *Annual Report*, 1954-55, p. 3.

32. Despite the Justice Department's reprieve, Davies was later dismissed from the Foreign Service on grounds of "lack of judgment, discretion and reliability"; see *New York Times*, November 6, 1954.

terests" to his denial that he had known "Asiaticus" as a Communist. However, no indictment tested Lattimore's denial of Budenz' charge that he had been a Communist.[33]

After the issuance of the indictment, Lattimore was given leave with pay by his employer, Johns Hopkins University, until the court had reached its decision. Lattimore, with the help of many friends, quickly organized a vigorous defense, both in and out of court. Friends secured numerous testimonials about Lattimore's scholarship,[34] while Lattimore's lawyers sought to have the indictment quashed by United States District Judge Luther Youngdahl. Decisions by Judge Youngdahl and the District Court of Appeals dismissed two counts, generally on grounds that the indictments were too vague. With the heart of its case taken away, the government decided to seek a new indictment. A new two-count charge was secured, but Judge Youngdahl dismissed both counts and was upheld by the Court of Appeals on a tie vote.[35] After assessing the matter, the Justice Department on June 18, 1955, announced it was ending its effort to convict Lattimore of perjury.[36] Thus, the courts were spared the opportunity of examining the evidence on even some of the more minor conflicts in the testimony of Lattimore and his accusers.

While the conclusion of Lattimore's court case was certainly a victory for himself and for the IPR, it is unlikely that the resultant sparse publicity was adequate to change significantly the IPR's public image. In many ways the organization's past continued to haunt it. In 1955, even among the academic community, the IPR's cause was not universally championed. Political scientist H. Bradford Westerfield, in writing his *Foreign Policy and Party Politics,* had this to say about the institute:

No brief summary here can do justice to the massive weight of evidence accumulated by the McCarran Committee during its long investigation in 1951 and 1952. By the standards reasonably

33. Ibid., December 17, 1952. See also U.S. Court of Appeals, District of Columbia Circuit, *U.S.A.* v. *Owen Lattimore,* No. 111849 (1954).

34. George Boas and Harvey Wheeler, eds., *Lattimore the Scholar* (Baltimore: 1953).

35. *New York Times,* October 8, 1954.

36. Ibid., June 29, 1955.

applicable to congressional probes, this one was conscientious and productive. Its 5,000 pages of testimony, with extensive and orderly documentation, deserve more respectful attention than they have received from most liberal critics, many of whom have not even bothered to read the committee's 200-page report. Unfortunately, there is room here only to state a personal conclusion: that a Communist solution for Asia was favored by a large enough proportion of the active partiticipants in the American IPR to affect substantially the content of its publications and the character of its public relations work and contacts with government.[37]

Thus, by mid-1955 the Institute of Pacific Relations had successfully avoided the dissolution which seemed so inevitable in late 1953. However, its financial base was fragile and its good reputation continued to be tarnished by its past. It was at this point that government again affected the fortunes of the IPR.

Internal Revenue Delivers a Blow

In retrospect, 1955 can be seen as a swing year in American history, one in which the political climate of the early fifties had begun to alter. But the process had just begun, and Washington still contained a number of key offfiicials who were sympathetic to the McCarthy movement. One such official was T. Coleman Andrews, a friend of Senator McCarthy and commissioner of Internal Revenue.

On May 26, 1955, the International IPR received a letter from Andrews stating that its tax exemption—the lifeblood for many nonprofit organizations—was being revoked retroactive to January 1 of the same year. Andrews alleged that the IPR had pursued its objectives by other than educational means and had "engaged in the dissemination of controversial and partisan propaganda. . . . " He also asserted that the IPR had attempted to influence the activities of government officials. Two months later, the AIPR's exemption was revoked on the grounds that it was "dependent" on the international group.[38]

Recognizing that a long and costly court case would

37. Westerfield, *Foreign Policy and Party Politics*, p. 246.
38. See T. Coleman Andrews to IPR, May 25, 1955, Vancouver Files; "Statement by Pacific Institute on Loss of Tax Exemption," October 18, 1955, Columbia Files.

severely strain the IPR's finances, institute leaders at first sought to gain administrative remedy. After a certain amount of delay, an informal meeting was arranged for August 16, 1955, at the Treasury Department. However, IPR representatives at the session found the Treasury officials unwilling to give them a bill of particulars for the IRS action. The IPR representatives came away with the impression that Commissioner Andrews had probably initiated the revocation and thus his subordinates were unwilling to become very deeply involved in the matter without his acceptance.[39]

Several other efforts were made to gain administrative remedy, but all failed. By mid-1956 the IPR's attorney recommended that the institute file suit in the Federal District Court of New York before the end of July 20. The decision to sue was at last made, and the suit began its tortuous route through the courts. At one point William Holland informed his attorney that the IPR might have to drop the case for lack of funds, but in the end this did not prove necessary.[40]

The institute's court efforts were fully vindicated on March 31, 1960, in a ruling by District Judge David N. Edelstein. After examining the sole exhibit presented by the government—the McCarran Committee report—Judge Edelstein concluded that there was not a "scintilla of evidence" to meet the defendant's case for the year 1955, the year in which the IRS had revoked the IPR's exemption.[41] Thus, the courts had agreed with a major IPR criticism of the McCarran Committee—its failure to depict the institute as it was, not as it had been.

The Road to Dissolution

While the tax ruling was being contested, the institute, and especially the AIPR, was forced to undertake some detailed thinking about its future. The seriousness of the situation

39. "Report on Conference with Bureau of Internal Revenue," undated, Vancouver Files.

40. AIPR, Minutes of Annual Meeting of Board of Trustees, June 27, 1957, Columbia Files.

41. Decision of Court, United States District Court, Southern District of New York, *Institute of Pacific Relations* v. *United States of America*, March 31, 1960.

which faced the AIPR in the aftermath of the IRS decision was made crystal clear in late 1955, when the Board of Trustees resolved a tight budget problem only by underpaying the AIPR's yearly grant to the Pacific Council.[42] The cash balance of the AIPR was dramatically drawn down in 1956, and the proposed budget for 1957 was only about twenty-six thousand dollars, a long step downward from its wartime heyday, when the budget was almost three hundred thousand dollars. By mid-1957 membership in the American IPR stood at 371, down from a peak of 2,000 in 1945.[43] Although the AIPR had been able to keep alive a small program, it was obvious to the trustees that the whole question of the future of the organization would have to be re-examined.

Two forms of rescue efforts were attempted. In the first, informal inquiries were made to see whether the Asia Society, a new Rockefeller-funded organization concerned mainly with Asian cultural matters, would be willing to take over the functions of the IPR. This proposal, like many others during the 1950's, was unsuccessful.[44] Next, a special membership and fund-raising campaign was announced, but that, too, was inadequate. By late 1957 Holland was forced to suggest some possible solutions to the problems facing the whole IPR. Among his suggestions were a more limited program, or even movement of the Secretariat to a location outside the United States. He recommended that any decisions be held off until the next IPR conference to be held at Lahore.[45] When the Pacific Council meeting convened at Lahore, the British delegate favored dissolution. However, no decision was taken.[46]

42. AIPR, Minutes of Executive Committee Meeting, November 27, 1955. Vancouver Files.

43. AIPR, *Biennial Report*, 1944-46, p. 46; AIPR, *Annual Report*, 1956-57, p. 7

44. AIPR, *Annual Report*, 1956-57, p. 2. The lack of success was attributed to the desire of the Asia Society to keep its program strictly in the social and cultural fields. In addition, of course, in the political climate of 1956 few American organizations wished to risk a public association with the IPR.

45. William L. Holland, "Memorandum on the Future of the IPR," November 19, 1957, Vancouver Files.

46. Minutes of Pacific Council Meeting, April 9, 1960, Vancouver Files.

By 1960, despite its victory in the tax case, the IPR could no longer postpone a decision. No new sources of financing had been found and it was apparent that quick action would be needed to salvage even a portion of the IPR's program. An opportunity soon presented itself. The University of British Columbia, which was looking for a chairman of its Asian Studies department, offered Holland the position. In addition, the university indicated a willingness to publish *Pacific Affairs* and to continue some of the publication and distribution work then carried on by the IPR. By October, both Holland and the Pacific Council had decided to accept this arrangement and to close the IPR's New York office by the end of the year.[47]

Since the AIPR had long shared offices with the International Secretariat, the former was also faced with an immediate decision about its future. Since no feasible plan had been found to revive the AIPR, its leaders directed their concern toward preserving its one remaining substantial program— *Far Eastern Survey*. This was achieved when the University of California at Berkeley offered to provide a home for the *Survey*.[48]

What remained was only the formal dissolution of the Pacific Council and the AIPR. The process was delayed briefly in order to complete negotiations with the Internal Revenue Service on the return of tax-exempt status to the two organizations. When these had been successfully concluded, the IPR could claim a victory over its opponents even when conceding its inability to survive. By October 1961, the long journey was over; both the Pacific Council and the AIPR had voted to dissolve.

During its thirty-six years, the Institute of Pacific Relations had been a pioneer in developing private Western contacts with Asia. In its first two decades it had been an important force in expanding research in an underdeveloped field. When

47. Holland to the AIPR trustees, August 22, 1960, Vancouver Files. See also "Notes on the IPR," undated, Vancouver Files.
48. Since 1961, California has published the new journal, *Asian Survey*. It should be noted that both in content and in internal procedures for evaluating manuscripts, *Asian Survey* differs significantly from *Far Eastern Survey*.

World War II brought the United States with a rush into the conflicts of the Far East, America and Americans were probably somewhat better prepared as the result of the work of the IPR. But in the decade which followed, the institute experienced great difficulty in adjusting its programs to a changing field of American Asian studies. At the same time, the IPR was unable to cope with fundamental elements in the American political system—elements made stronger by a series of events both at home and in Asia.

In retrospect, it can be said that the IPR had taken sick by 1947; by 1953 it was gravely ill. By 1961 the story of the IPR was a moot question for most Americans. But the issues involved in the IPR's decline and fall are not dead. They have continued to have immense significance for both Asian studies and America's foreign and domestic policies. With the perspective of a tumultuous decade, it is possible to begin an assessment of that significance.

6

The IPR Affair and Far Eastern Studies in the United States

ANYONE attempting to assess the significance of the IPR case for America's Far Eastern studies should at the outset acknowledge the difficulties of such a task. To begin with, it is very difficult to isolate phenomena which directly concerned the IPR from general political phenomena as causal elements resulting in some kind of impact on American specialists on the Far East. For example, some Far Eastern specialists may have been much more concerned with the actions of their college board of trustees or state legislatures than with the McCarran Committee's investigation of the IPR. For others, the latter investigation may have had much greater impact.

It is perhaps best to begin by examining evidence relating to the impact of the McCarthy period on scholars generally. When the general picture is established, the spotlight can then be focused on the more particular case of Asian scholars. At first glance it would appear that the American academic community was vitally affected by the domestic political climate during the first part of the 1950's. Such concern was amply demonstrated during 1949-54 by the *Bulletin* of the American Association of University Professors (AAUP). During that time virtually every issue of the *Bulletin* contained an article expressing concern for the future of academic freedom. Leading spokesmen for the academic community frequently indicated their alarm about the impact of the political climate upon freedom of inquiry. At one point, an eminent historian claimed that the politicians of the moment were attempting to promote a new loyalty, which "demands uncritical and unquestioning acceptance of America as it is —the political institutions, the social relationships, the economic practices."[1] By 1954, a well-known educator was asserting that "the entire teaching profession of the United States is now intimidated."[2] A straw poll by *The New York Times* found college teachers reluctant to speak out on controversial issues, cautious about joining political clubs, and wary of potential legislative investigations.[3]

Clearly, there was some substance to these concerns. Between 1948 and 1954, the AAUP reported a steadily increasing number of cases involving claimed violations in regulations concerning academic freedom and tenure. The heavy increase in such cases was prompted not only by matters resulting from state and federal loyalty investigations but also from professorial resistance to state legislatures, which enacted a variety of loyalty oaths which were made mandatory elements of contracts for teachers in some state-run colleges and universities.

When the record is examined for hard evidence, however, it seems equally true that the concerns of professors during the early 1950's can be overplayed. Despite its own increasing attention to the matter, the AAUP reported that out of faculties with a total of about 180,000 teachers, probably only sixty or seventy teachers had been dismissed at a total of twenty-five or thirty schools.[4]

Perhaps the most thorough study of teachers' concerns was revealed in 1955 by social scientists Paul Lazarfield and Wagner Thielens. Their poll of some twenty-five hundred college and university social scientists showed that a majority felt that increased public concern over the opinions and politi-

1. Henry Steele Commager, *Freedom, Loyalty, Dissent* (New York: Oxford University Press, 1954), p. 142.

2. Robert M. Hutchins, "Are Our Teachers Afraid to Teach?", *AAUP Bulletin*, 40 (Summer 1954): 205.

3. *New York Times*, May 11, 1951.

4. Ralph F. Fuchs, "Intellectual Freedom and the Educational Process," *AAUP Bulletin*, 42 (Autumn 1956): 476. Fuchs did not clarify the extent to which factors other than academic ones may have been involved in the dismissals.

cal persuasions of teachers had been harmful to a climate of freedom in the country. But by almost four to one they asserted that their own academic freedom had not been threatened. Although about half of the respondents said they had been criticized for joining a controversial group or supporting an unpopular cause, very few believed their own academic career had been adversely affected. A large majority believed that their social science colleagues were not avoiding controversial subjects because of the political climate, although a significant minority dissented on this point. The poll also showed that anxiety levels among college professors were highly skewed; that is, social scientists who were "highly permissive" felt much more apprehension than those who were "clearly conservative."[5]

THE SPLIT AMONG ASIAN SCHOLARS

Having glimpsed the attitudes of professors as a whole, it is now possible to examine in somewhat more detail the specific impact of the period, and especially the McCarran investigation, on Asian scholars. The first major effect is difficult to measure but very real: a deepening bitterness between individual members in the field holding differing political and historical views. The McCarran hearings, and especially the testimony of some of the more "conservative" Asian scholars, produced a period of strained and awkward relationships among members of the field. In a few cases, divisions were so deep that people simply ceased speaking with each other. More often, however, the effects could be measured in less dramatic ways. For example, a professor might be appointed to a committee or a panel primarily on the grounds that it was thought advisable to include a recognizable "conservative" in the field. On the other hand, one "conservative" member of the field believed that he had lost his position at one university as a result of his strong views on the IPR.[6]

5. Paul F. Lazarfield and Wagner Thielens, Jr., *The Academic Mind* (Glencoe, Ill.: Free Press, 1958), pp. 35, 114-19, 153, 378-84. "Highly permissive" professors were defined as those who were willing to tolerate in certain forms Communist groups or teachers on campus.
6. After his dismissal, the scholar in question was told by another scholar, "Well, we finally got ———."

Only rarely did the tensions among Asian scholars break into print in academic literature. An exception was the vigorous and acrimonious debate conducted in the *China Quarterly* in 1960 by Sinologists Karl Wittfogel and Benjamin Schwartz. After Wittfogel had charged him with showing unconcern over "mounting evidence" against his interpretation of the Chinese Communist movement, Schwartz probably spoke for most members of the field when he replied:

For some years now Prof. Wittfogel has been obsessed with the view that Fairbank, Schwartz and Brandt (an indivisible entity) have committed an "error" (not an accidental error!) which has led to incalculably evil results in our struggle with world Communism.[7]

Continuing with his rebuttal, Schwartz concluded on a theme of basic respect among scholars:

In dealing with the obscure story of Chinese Communism, we have all committed errors. Prof. Wittfogel's evidence will have to "mount" much higher than it has till now, however, before I become convinced that I have committed the particular errors which he ascribed to me. It is in fact high time that Prof. Wittfogel overcame the illusion that his particular experiences and his particular "theories" vouchsafe for him some peculiar access to an understanding of Communism not available to the rest of us. His views of Communist history may be right or wrong. They do not stem from any higher source than the views of the rest of us.[8]

Job security is a second area in which one can assess the impact of the McCarran Committee investigation. While concrete information is difficult to obtain,[9] one conclusion seems apparent: those professors and researchers who denied the accusations of Communist ties received a high degree of protection from their employers. Following his indictment on perjury charges, Owen Lattimore was given leave *with pay* by his employer, Johns Hopkins University. John Fairbank

7. Benjamin Schwartz, "The Legend of the 'Legend of "Maoism,"'" *China Quarterly*, 2 (April-June 1960): 35. See also Karl Wittfogel, "The Legend of 'Maoism,'" Ibid., 1 (January-March 1960): 77-86; and 2 (April-June 1960): 16-34.

8. Schwartz, "The Legend of the 'Legend of "Maoism,"'" *China Quarterly*, 2 (April-June 1960): 242.

9. The American Association of University Professors has informed the author that its confidential files on academic freedom and tenure from that period are not yet available to researchers (William P. Fidler to the author, February 1, 1971).

was retained by Harvard despite the charges made against him by Louis Budenz. Many other IPR personalities were similarly retained in their positions despite efforts by the committee to imply that they had participated in "pro-Communist" activities. As for those who invoked their fifth amendment privileges during the hearings, the record is less clear. In at least one case, however, it appears that a promising writer and researcher (Lawrence Rosinger) was forced to give up his career as a result of his decision to take the fifth amendment.

In terms of the government's relationship with Asian scholars, the picture is less favorable, although in most cases negative patterns proved fleeting. For example, in 1953 David L. Shillinglaw's appointment to the United Nations Economic and Social Council was blocked by the Senate, apparently because of his membership in the IPR. At one one point in the early 1950's, ex-San Francisco Bay Secretary Eugene Staley experienced difficulty in obtaining a government security clearance, presumably because of his IPR connections.[10] The matter was later resolved, however, and Staley was ultimately given a vital role in researching and writing an important government report on suggestions for American economic policy toward Vietnam.[11]

EFFECTS ON RESEARCH AND PUBLISHING

Aside from the personal impact on members of the field, there is the important question of how the period and the demise of the IPR affected American research and publications related to East Asia. Again, it is necessary to begin with a warning. Some judgments can be made about what was published. However, it is much more difficult to say what would have been published in the absence of political pressures in Congress and public opinion. In addition, many factors affect a scholar's ability to write. In some years his health and fam-

10. Lynn White, Jr., to Eugene Staley, May 30, 1952, McLaughlin Papers.

11. The "Staley Plan" advocated establishment of "strategic hamlets" in South Vietnam as a means of consolidating government control against Vietcong forces. See George McTurnan Kahin and John W. Lewis, *The United States in Vietnam* (New York: Dial Press, 1967), pp. 128, 282.

ily problems may be just as important to a reduction of output as the political criteria of publishers. When the matter is examined in detail, it is apparent that the subject is complex and must be broken down into several parts.

Clearly there was no obvious cut-off in research or publication on East Asia or China. From 1951 to 1955, during the height of the McCarthy period, a large volume of original work was published. A number of these works are still recognized as important contributions to the field. They include *The United States and Japan* by Edwin Reischauer, Harold Vinacke's *the United States and the Far East,* and *The China Tangle* by Herbert Feis. Perhaps even more significantly, the literature of the early 1950's contains three important works authored or co-edited by John Fairbank, the most noted Asian scholar to be accused of Communist ties by Louis Budenz during the McCarran hearings. These works are *Trade and Diplomacy on the China Coast, China's Response to the West,* and *A Documentary History of Chinese Communism.* (For further discussion of Fairbank's treatment by American publishers, see below.)

Despite these evidences of health in American scholarship during the early 1950's, a reviewer can also conclude that something was missing in volumes dealing with the political aspects of Communist China. In particular, the major American works of the fifties presented a viewpoint about China's internal politics and foreign relations which later proved overly rigid. In the mid-1950's, Richard Walker's depiction of the Chinese Communist political system as a case study of totalitarianism seemed apt; [12] later research, however, suggests that such a model was too inflexible.[13] In foreign relations, the dominant books of the period often expressed a view of the stability of the Sino-Soviet alliance which was quickly overcome by the events of the sixties.[14]

12. See Richard L. Walker, *China under Communism: The First Five Years* (New Haven, Conn.: Yale University Press, 1955).

13. See, for example, Parris H. Chang, "Research Notes on the Changing Loci of Decision in the CCP," *China Quarterly,* 44 (October-December 1970): 169-94.

14. Books by Paul Linebarger and Peter Tang expressed complete confidence about the solidarity of the Sino-Soviet alliance. See Paul

This is not to suggest that the works listed above resulted from the political climate of the times. However, the relative absence of authoritative American political science works taking a more flexible view is surprising, especially in view of the differing attitudes on these questions by American writers during the 1940's. A reasonable hypothesis is that both American writers and publishers were wary of identifying themselves with more "liberal" interpretations of China's politics and foreign policy during the early 1950's, especially while the Korean conflict continued.

The sections above have considered mainly how scholarly, book-length publications fared during the controversies of the early 1950's. A different picture can be obtained by looking at the impact of contributions by individual Asian scholars to the popular press. One facet of the issue has been discussed by Ross Koen, who found that several Asian scholars accused of Communist ties during the McCarran Committee investigation had appeared frequently as reviewers in the book review columns of the *New York Times* and the *New York Herald Tribune* during 1945 and 1950. From 1952 to 1956, Koen found that many of the same writers were missing from such spaces.[15]

The impact on popular writing is revealed sharply in the cases of individual writers. Prior to 1950, Owen Lattimore was an amazingly prolific writer, in both popular and specialist journals. Following the accusations made against him by Senator McCarthy and others, however, Lattimore's writing quickly became a scarce commodity, even in specialist journals. By the mid-1950's his writings no

---

Linebarger, *Far Eastern Governments and Politics* (New York: Van Nostrand, 1954), p. 251, and Peter S. H. Tang, *Communist China Today* (New York: Praeger, 1957). Books by W. W. Rostow and Howard Boorman were less dogmatic on this subject, although both concluded that a Sino-Soviet split was unlikely. Rostow prefaced his work by indicating his belief that Communist China was basically a danger in need of containment by the West. See Walt W. Rostow, ed., *The Prospects for Communist China* (New York: John Wiley & Sons, 1954). See also Howard L. Boorman, ed., *Moscow-Peking Axis: Strengths and Strains* (New York: Harper, 1957), p. 51.

15. See Ross Y. Koen, *The China Lobby in American Politics*, p. 151.

longer appeared in American journals.[16] Prior to 1950, Lattimore had also produced a variety of books for American publishers on subjects ranging from Mongolia to American policy on the Far East. After 1950, it is necessary to wait until 1968 to find an American-published book by Lattimore.

A similar, although less vivid, result emerges from an examination of articles written by John Fairbank. In 1949-1950 Fairbank authored six articles including several for journals which cannot properly be termed "liberal." Between April 1951 and February 1957, the *Reader's Guide* lists only two popular articles by Fairbank, both for liberally oriented journals. Although Fairbank continued to write occasional articles in his field, his "rehabilitation" by the American popular press did not come until 1966, when *Life* commissioned him to write a feature story on China. Fairbank's relative absence from popular literature during the fifties and early sixties illustrates his comment that some Asian scholars "lost the demand for our services" during that period.[17]

There is little doubt regarding one long-range trend affecting research and publishing on East Asia during the 1950's. The period produced a striking shift away from activity dependent on one Asian studies organization (the IPR) to research and publishing efforts associated with the budding American university Asian research centers. It would be inaccurate to say that this movement was a result of the political climate or congressional investigations; by the late 1940's the major American foundations had already decided to switch their funds from the IPR to university centers. However, this process was accelerated by politics, since the political climate quickened the institute's demise. Other factors should be cited, however. As the 1950's wore on, university presses greatly increased their capabilities, and commercial presses increased their willingness, to publish books on East Asia.

In a number of ways, the field's new diversity was a blessing. It offered young scholars increased opportunity to publish

16. The *Reader's Guide* lists only three articles by Lattimore during the 1951-54 period and none from 1955-60.

17. *Newsweek*, 73 (April 14, 1969): 74.

their research. At the same time, it granted the field greater immunity from political pressures, since greater diversity meant that congressmen could no longer claim that one organization dominated research and writing about East Asia. An additional factor was that university presses had their own schools and often state pride behind them.

In one important respect, it is likely that political pressures—or at least concern for political pressures by foundations and universities—brought about a curious anomaly in one segment of American Asian studies. Although government and private money was poured into the development of Chinese studies during the 1950's, no scholarly journal devoted exclusively to modern China was established in the United States. In 1960, this vacuum was filled by the London-based *China Quarterly*. To this day, that journal remains the principal journal for scholarly writing about modern China.

EFFECTS ON THE ORGANIZATION OF ASIAN STUDIES

As previously noted, the weakening and eventual demise of the IPR took place at a time when American Asian studies as a whole were experiencing a period of rapid expansion. In addition, for some time many American scholars had felt that the IPR, with its international emphasis and biennial global conferences, did not fit their needs. Thus, it was likely that American Asian specialists would seek a new focus for organizing their field.

Such a focus did not appear all at once. Neither should its development be seen as a conscious effort on the part of leaders in the field to provide a successor to the IPR. The process began in 1948 because Far Eastern scholars in the American Oriental Society felt a need for their own professional organization and doubted that the structure of the AOS could be changed to meet their needs.[18] While some consideration was given to working within a revitalized IPR, this idea was not taken up for two reasons. The first was that the

18. This account is based on Karl J. Pelzer, "Notes from the Desk of the President of the Association for Asian Studies," *AAS Newsletter*, 12 (December 1966): 11. The American Oriental Society is an organization set up to promote research and publication in Oriental languages, literature, history, and art.

organizers disliked the IPR's structure of national councils. Secondly, in the back of their minds was a vague uneasiness about the past leadership and future potential of the IPR.[19] At the initiative of the Committee on Far Eastern Studies of the American Council of Learned Societies, a number of Asian scholars met and decided to establish the Far Eastern Association. The *Far Eastern Quarterly*, a publication which had existed independently since the early 1940's, became its journal.

It seems likely that even in the absence of political currents affecting Asian studies, the idea of a professional Asian studies organization would have appealed to many American academicians. However, the IPR's decline gave the new organization a special attractiveness. Foundations, which found it expedient to avoid the IPR, began to show interest in the Far Eastern Association.

From the outset the new organization attempted to avoid the political pitfalls which had helped weaken the IPR. On the whole, the *Far Eastern Quarterly* stressed historical studies in preference to questions of current controversy. In addition, it avoided the editorials (or semi-editorials) which occasionally appeared in the *Far Eastern Survey* during this period.

However, the Far Eastern Association could not avoid facing the concerns of some of its leading members that America's political climate was adversely affecting Asian studies. Thus, at its 1952 meeting, the FEA adopted a strongly worded resolution stating that Far Eastern research was being endangered because of partisan attacks and fear of reprisals. It deplored efforts to enforce conformity and orthodoxy in the field and attacks upon the motives and character of specialists or their associations. It also criticized arbitrary limitations on travel.[20] In the broadest sense, of course, the resolution was not "nonpolitical." However, its scope and wording was praised by "conservatives" as well as "liberals" in the field.[21]

19. Claude Buss, personal interview, March 16, 1971.

20. William Theodore de Bary, "The Association for Asian Studies: Nonpolitical but not Unconcerned," *Journal of Asian Studies*, 29 (August 1970): 754-55.

21. See Richard L. Walker, "Prof. Walker Replies," *New Leader*, 35 (April 21, 1952): 10-11.

THE ASSOCIATION FOR ASIAN STUDIES

By 1957, the IPR was tottering on its last legs. In contrast, the Far Eastern Association was prospering amid the general expansion of the field. In that year, the FEA took on a new name, the Association for Asian Studies (AAS), and titled its publication the *Journal of Asian Studies*. By 1958 its membership had risen to twelve hundred.

During the better part of its first decade, the Association for Asian Studies was able to avoid the political controversies which plagued the IPR. There were a few dissenting voices when, in 1958 and 1961, the association went on record as affirming the need for maximum scholarly contacts with all of Asia and supporting President John F. Kennedy's efforts to prevent any delay in delivery of foreign printed matter to Americans.[22] Generally, however, the AAS was more concerned with the problems of adapting itself to a much larger and more specialized field of study than it was at dealing with questions related to government or politics.

By the early 1960's the AAS, by adhering to a scholarly and nonpolitical stance, had helped to mellow some of the tension and bitterness which had existed a decade earlier in the Asian studies field. Some personal animosities were eased over time, and research prospered. The controversies of the past seemed to be abating in a larger and more diversified field.

This surface calm was, however, shattered by the reaction of professors and students to America's deepening involvement in Vietnam. Within two years after President Kennedy's decision to send advisers to that land, America found itself engaged in a large-scale, costly, and confusing war in Asia. The nature of the conflict posed moral dilemmas much more acute than Asian specialists had yet confronted. The longer the war continued, the more pressure it placed on professors and students to take a political stand. At the same time, its existence placed heavy pressures on the field. Graduate students and young professors clashed with their elders and began to re-examine the whole fabric of thought in the field. Among the more emotional, there were cries that the research of veteran Asian scholars had merely provided intellectual

22. *AAS Newsletter*, 4 (May 1959): 4; 6 (May 1961): 2.

underpinnings for the government's war effort. As the major organization of Asian scholars, the AAS could not avoid dealing with such concerns.

By 1966 pressures on the AAS to take a political stand had increased to the point where association president Karl Pelzer felt compelled to mention his concern and objections. Pelzer mentioned two instances in which the association's name had been used without authority to enhance political statements about America's Asian policy. He also took some pains to refute claims by an Ohio Congressman that the AAS was a successor to the IPR, pointing out that the AAS constitution, its desire to maintain tax-exempt status, and other factors all argued against its participation in political activities.[23]

By 1968 the concerns of many younger scholars, as well as the refusal of the AAS to bend to political pressures, brought about a difficult situation. It appeared that meetings of the AAS, like those of several other scholarly organizations, might be the target of disruptions by angry students and professors. That this did not happen was largely the decision of younger activists to concentrate their energies outside of the AAS. In 1968 a group of students and professors met to form the Committee of Concerned Asian Scholars (CCAS).[24] From the beginning, the CCAS was the antithesis of the AAS. Openly political in nature, the CCAS quickly organized "counterconventions" to meetings of the AAS featuring panels devoted to "relevant" topics and business sessions which passed resolutions condemning United States actions in Indochina.[25]

At its annual meeting in 1969, the AAS made one small concession to the concerns of its more activist members by permitting a special panel discussion on "The Effects of the McCarran Hearings on China Studies." Organized by Richard Kagen, a Harvard graduate student and CCAS leader, the panel included talks by former State Department China

23. *AAS Newsletter*, 12 (December 1966): 7-12.

24. In its beginning stages, CCAS was supported by a number of recognized Asian specialists, including John Fairbank, Mary Wright, and Marc Mancall.

25. See below for a more extensive discussion of the structure and activities of the CCAS.

specialist O. Edmund Clubb; Ross Koen, author of a book about the "China Lobby"; Owen Lattimore; and Howard Zinn, radical professor and political activist at Boston University.

In many ways, the panel illustrated trends in some segments of American scholarship.[26] To begin with, the panelists were of one mind about the impact of the McCarran hearings. Taken together, the discussions shed little light on the problems facing the scholar or policy-maker as a result of the legacy of the early 1950's. Rather, the listener was offered a series of reminiscences about the harms of the period from several individuals who had been deeply affected by it. Little effort was made to explain the difficulties of assessing the impact of the McCarran hearings as distinguished from other causal agents. One of the speakers, in assessing the impact of the period on America's Asian policy, failed to include factors independent of the domestic political climate, including such important events as the Korean War. The same speaker, in calling for a fundamental reappraisal of American policy, provided no appreciation of the current problems which would have to be faced in implementing such a reappraisal.

In a subdued fashion, the panel also revealed the dichotomies which existed among scholars calling for more activist opposition to American involvement in Indochina. Generally speaking, the "old liberals" on the panel (Koen, Clubb, and Lattimore) concentrated their fire on past injustices. The "New Left" representatives, Kagen and Zinn, asked that specific actions be carried out immediately by the AAS and other parties. Kagan called upon the AAS to take a more aggressive attitude on public matters and warned Asian scholars not to avoid involvement with large segments of the public. Zinn derided the association's lack of "relevance," questioned the efficacy of normal political processes, and called for direct action by the people.

For the most part, the audience, heavily populated by students from the Boston area, responded warmly to the speakers. Like some campus "discussion" meetings the

26. This analysis is based on the author's notes of the session.

author has recently attended, the atmosphere more closely resembled that of a united political group rather than a scholarly gathering which seeks to examine many sides of a question and encourages an audience to participate in such a process. Whether the audience was bothered by the atmosphere at the session is not clear. However, during the question period one prominent Asian specialist, Benjamin Schwartz of Harvard, rose to express his concern that too great an emphasis on "relevance" could lead to significant problems of anti-intellectualism.

Despite the decision of the CCAS leaders to concentrate their political actions outside of the AAS, pressures on the AAS to take a political stance did not end. After taking soundings at several regional meetings, AAS president William Theodore De Bary took up the subject at the 1970 AAS convention. De Bary began by noting that the new AAS constitution reaffirmed the original document in stating that the organization was nonpolitical. The AAS need not be unconcerned, he thought, but ought to limit its public stands to matters directly within its responsibility, such as threats to the free pursuit of knowledge or to basic educational functions of scholarship. He believed that the association had no direct responsibility for matters of foreign policy or national defense. De Bary cited the 1952 resolution of the Far Eastern Association as proper and still valid for 1970. The major purpose of the association, he believed, was to provide a forum for discussion and dissemination of information about Asia. To take a stand on public issues would compromise its openness and undercut the association's past success in bringing together persons of divergent political views for advances of knowledge in the field.[27]

While De Bary emphasized that his speech should be considered a personal view, it seems very likely that his remarks would be endorsed by a majority of AAS members. Despite the concerns of some of its members that the association is too stodgy and conservative for the times, the AAS can point to one important achievement. It has become the major focus

27. De Bary, "The Association for Asian Studies: Nonpolitical but not Unconcerned," pp. 751-59.

of American scholarly activity in the Asian field and has avoided temptations which might have brought it troubles similar to those encountered by the IPR.[28]

Of course, in many senses the AAS is not comparable to the IPR, since it has no national councils, does not maintain a research staff of its own, and does not involve itself in community education programs. Nevertheless, the success of the AAS in avoiding America's political shoals has also resulted from its clarity of goals and the strength and quality of its elected leadership. From the beginning, the leaders of the Far Eastern Association had a clear idea about the purposes of their organization. Despite rapid growth and the pressure of the times, this path has been successfully maintained.

THE COMMITTEE OF CONCERNED ASIAN SCHOLARS

No analysis of modern Asian studies organizations would be complete without a fuller discussion of the CCAS. The Concerned Asian Scholars not only provide organizational testimony to the frustrations of young professors and students with America's Asian policies and its traditional scholarly organizations. The existence of CCAS also is a product of the scope and diversity in modern American Asian studies.

From its inception, the CCAS has openly affirmed its political emphasis as an organization dedicated to changing America's Asian policies. It has stressed the point that scholars "bear responsibility for the consequences of their research and the political posture of their profession." Nationally, CCAS sees itself as a catalyst and coordinator for the development of "anti-imperialist" research.[29]

Unlike the AAS or the IPR, the Concerned Asian Scholars have taken clear-cut positions on foreign policy issues. At the 1969 CCAS national conference, for example, delegates adopted resolutions opposing continuation of the United States-Japan Security Treaty, and calling for immediate withdrawal

28. Other scholarly organizations have not been so strong in their resistance to political pressures. In 1971, the Modern Language Association endorsed a "people's peace treaty" with the Vietnamese people; see *Newsweek*, 77 (January 11, 1971): 58.

29. CCAS, "Statement of Purpose (National)," undated mimeograph.

of United States forces from Vietnam as well as American support for a coalition government in South Vietnam. A resolution was adopted urging American diplomatic recognition of the People's Republic of China.[30]

The National CCAS provides general support to local chapters and organizes national conventions. It also edits the organization's journal, the *Bulletin of the Concerned Asian Scholars*. While articles in the *Bulletin* reflect the political orientation of CCAS, in recent times they have occasionally shown a rather surprising degree of research and thoroughness.[31] Nationally, CCAS supports itself with individual donations and profits from writings by its members.

Individual chapters on college campuses provide the major focus for CCAS activities. In 1970 there were roughly fifteen chapters, mostly at large and prestigious universities which have significant graduate programs in Asian studies. A quick look at the activities of the Stanford chapter during 1969-70 provides a capsule view of CCAS at work. The Stanford CCAS organized films, lectures, and social events, usually with an anti-war theme. It sponsored frequent discussion meetings for its members and provided speakers on Asia for local high schools and civic groups. During 1969 the Stanford chapter played an active role in the October 15 Mobilization. During 1970 it actively supported the national student strike to protest the United States incursion into Cambodia. The political makeup of the Stanford chapter CCAS varied from liberal to radical. For the most part, members were united only in their opposition to the war and their concern over the moral responsibilities of research.

There are perils, of course, in attempting to summarize the history of an organization in its fifth year. The organizational structure and work of the CCAS are as yet very fluid, and predictions about its future course would of necessity be highly tentative. Nevertheless, as of early 1973 it can be said that the Committee of Concerned Asian

30. Ibid.
31. *China Quarterly* editor David Wilson told one group of students he wished some *Bulletin* articles had been offered to his journal.

Scholars has served as a valuable focus within which concerned and angry young students and professors can channel their energies. It has also lessened the frustrations which activist Asian specialists otherwise might have directed against the Association for Asian Studies.

Some important questions remain, however, concerning groups such as CCAS which attempt to fuse scholarship and politics. For example, can CCAS members, having once attempted to connect the roles of scholar and politician, separate them later when they take up teaching positions at colleges and universities? Of course, this question would exist whether or not there was a CCAS. Young students and professors today are increasingly concerned about the uses to which their research is put. If taken too far, such concerns can easily lead to biased scholarship, since an author may decide to avoid mentioning elements of a situation which could be distorted or quoted out of context to support a policy viewpoint which the author considers intolerable. Can the CCAS member mitigate his feelings in the classroom to the extent that he can create an atmosphere favorable to the presentation of many sides of view, even those he personally abhors? Can he, for example, discuss American involvement in Indochina in a manner which at least presents the major portions of the government's case? In the case of CCAS members, we do not yet have the answer to such questions.[32]

THE IMPACT ON FOREIGN POLICY

This study has examined how Asian studies organizations have handled certain key questions which affect their treatment by elements of the American political system. It has also been noted that strong feelings over foreign policy issues have had a major impact on Asian studies. In the case of the IPR, very difficult issues were posed by the Sino-Japanese conflict. Later, concerns over the proper degree of American aid for the Chinese Nationalists were

32. An additional consideration is the current depression-level state of employment opportunities in the Asian studies field, which may deprive many new Ph.D.'s, activists or not, of opportunities to undertake teaching as a career.

an important factor in initial charges linking the IPR with communism. Following the victory of the Chinese Communists, the IPR became a target for those in America calling for increased American aid to and identification with non-Communist Asian forces.

This study has not attempted to explore in any depth what implications the IPR case and the McCarthy period have had for foreign policy. Any definitive analysis of that issue would entail a separate study. Nevertheless, it does seem possible, from the material examined in this study, to re-examine some past theories and to offer some starting points for future research.

With the benefit of almost two decades' hindsight, it ought to be possible to initiate a refinement of some theories previously well received by East Asian specialists. One such theory is the assertion that a united and well-oiled "China lobby" successfully brought about a change in America's Asian policy by convincing the public that America's China specialists were tainted with pro-communism. In the words of Ross Koen, "It is fairly safe to say, in fact, that only the constant insistence that the writers and professional China specialists had been guilty of extensive 'Communist connections' enabled the China lobby to make an effective case for its attack on United States policy."[33]

Whether such a theory in its undiluted form was ever accurate should now be questioned. To begin with, it gives too little emphasis to the actions of Communist powers, especially Chinese entry into the Korean War and the hostile attitude of Chinese Communist officials to American consular representatives in China. In addition, a review of the activities of Alfred Kohlberg suggests that those opposed to the IPR did not always demonstrate great cohesion. In fact, Kohlberg's campaign against the IPR, widespread as it became, was largely a personal effort. It also seems dubious that the American public ever accepted the idea that Nationalist China was betrayed by disloyal American officials.[34]

33. Koen, *The China Lobby in American Politics*, p. 135.
34. A Gallup Poll taken in 1954 showed that only 7 percent of the

As time passes, it is increasingly possible to question the continued efficacy of the "China Lobby" theory as it applies to America's China policy. In 1973, it is very difficult to find even remnants of the "China Lobby." America's China policy is showing increasing flexibility and pragmatism; virtually all of the emotion which once characterized United States policy toward the Chinese Communists has been removed. De facto Sino-American diplomatic relations, an anathema to the "China Lobby," are now a reality.

Perhaps most interesting of all has been the contribution of Foreign Service officers to such changes. It could be hypothesized that harsh treatment of their predecessors during the early 1950's might have inclined present-day State Department China specialists towards timidity or at least excessive caution until very recently. From the author's own experience in the State Department, however, this has not been the case.[35]

Even in Indochina, America's heavy military involvement has been drawn down rapidly in accordance with the terms of the Vietnam peace settlement. American military action continued in Laos and Cambodia in early 1973, but at diminished levels. Even in those two fractious states, some form of negotiated settlement seemed possible.

Despite such recent flexibility in Asian policy, however, it cannot be disputed that American presidents from the 1950's onward have been willing to pay very heavy human and material costs and to take very high risks in an effort

---

respondents attributed the Nationalist defeat to such causes. Most cited Nationalist weaknesses as the key factor. George Gallup to the author, August 31. 1970.

35. This is not to say that Foreign Service officers have brought about a more flexible China policy today, any more than they were "responsible" for America's China policy during the 1940's. In both cases responsibility should be placed where it belongs—the President and his close advisers.

The impact of the McCarthy period on Foreign Service officers and State Department personnel may be tested in part when official reportage by such officials on Vietnam becomes available. Data from the recently publicized "Pentagon Papers" suggest that intelligence sources, including the State Department's Bureau of Intelligence and Research, often produced estimates at variance with the hopes of policy-makers. In addition, the Pentagon documents include a 1963

to prevent Communist successes in Asia. It must therefore be asked to what extent this involvement is a legacy of the early fifties. Obviously, the answer is complex and any theory which ignores such vital factors as chance happenings (assassinations) or presidential personalities would be incomplete. Nevertheless, there may be a common thread in American policy which needs closer examination. That is the concern of recent American presidents that an obvious "defeat" in Asia would result in an ugly reaction in America reminiscent of the McCarthy era.

Recent presidents have differed in the openness with which they have bared their thoughts on this issue. President Kennedy did not refer to it directly. However, former presidential assistant Kenneth O'Donnell has now stated that Kennedy planned to withdraw American advisers from Vietnam, but not until after the 1964 elections, since he feared the move might encourage a McCarthyist reaction at home.[36] Especially when the going in Vietnam got rough, President Lyndon B. Johnson was fond of reminding the public that he did not intend to be the first American president to preside over an American "defeat." President Richard M. Nixon has said the same thing and has often stated his concern that such a "defeat" would lead to harsh recriminations and divisions at home.

Whether such fears were justified is another subject

─────────

memo by former State Department Vietnam Affairs chief Paul Kattenburg recommending a pullout of U.S. advisers from Vietnam. See *New York Times*, June 13-15, 1971.

Even if the reporting of U.S. personnel in Saigon turns out to be overoptimistic about the progress of non-Communist forces, as the author suspects, several influences other than the impact of McCarthyism will require examination. These include the influence on reporting of senior officials as well as the beliefs of officers about the impact on their careers of political reporting which seems to undercut positions cherished by American presidents.

36. Kenneth O'Donnell, "LBJ and the Kennedys," *Life*, 69 (August 7, 1970): 51-52. Senate Majority Leader Mike Mansfield, who was present for most of the President's discussions with O'Donnell that day, has corroborated the main features of O'Donnell's account. O'Donnell states that Mansfield had left the room when the President expressed his concerns about a possible revival of McCarthyism. See *New York Times*, August 3, 1970.

requiring additional research. It is the author's view that just as congressmen overestimated their constituents' concerns with communism in the early 1950's, American presidents have exaggerated the degree to which Americans would react to an Asian setback. In particular, the author believes that additional research would suggest that such a reaction might well have small enough to allow successful handling by able presidential and congressional leadership.

7

The Congressional Process and Scholarly Groups: Some Observations from the IPR Case

THE preceding sections have described at length the manner in which the Institute of Pacific Relations came into conflict with elements in the American political system, especially Congress. On the basis of this study, what light can the IPR case shed on the procedures of congressional committees which conduct investigations involving scholarly and research organizations? In answering this question, it is necessary to discuss standards and definitions used by the McCarran Committee in an attempt to formulate some guideposts by which data could be evaluated in similar cases in the future. In addition, it is helpful to examine what issues the McCarran Committee avoided. These discussions can then lead to a more general consideration of issues such as loyalty, security, and academic freedom so strongly focused in the period as well as in the treatment of the Institute of Pacific Relations.

THE NATURE OF CONGRESSIONAL INVESTIGATIONS

Before discussing important features of the McCarran Committee's investigation of the IPR, it is worthwhile to review some generalizations about the American congressional investigatory committee. While the Constitution makes no specific reference to such activities by Congress, authority for congressional inquiries has been found in Article I, which states that "all legislative power herein granted shall be rested in a Congress. . . . " Few authorities have questioned the assertion that Congress, in order to seek facts for enacting legislation, to check the administration of laws, and perhaps even to disseminate information, does have the power to make investigations.[1]

What has been disputed, however, is the degree to which this power has been used, especially in investigations which seem only peripherally related to legislation. The nature of Congress itself has magnified such concerns. The congressional seniority system and the strong powers traditionally given committee chairmen have meant that the committees, and therefore congressional investigations, are often controlled by men unrepresentative of the nation and unresponsive to the national political parties. Senator McCarran is only one of many examples of this pattern. During the past several decades, congressional committees have been dominated by Southern Democrats, and less frequently, during times of Republican majorities, by Midwestern Republicans. In many cases, such men have brought rural or small-town attitudes to Washington. Often, as in the IPR case they have not shied from the use of congressional investigations as a means to defend such views or to attack ways of thought seen as inimical to the beliefs of their constituents.

In choosing committee staff members a chairman is likely to select men of his own persuasion. The outlook of staff members is crucial, since few congressmen or senators have the time to do the spade work necessary to conduct a congressional investigation. Even the questions which a congressman asks in a hearing are often the result of a suggestion from a committee staff member. As previously noted in the case of the McCarran Committee, the selection of a special subcommittee staff led by Robert Morris and Benjamin Mandel was an important factor in determining what sort of questions would be asked as well as what evidence would be introduced.

An additional factor which can lead to proliferating investigations is the lack of iron-clad divisions of responsi-

1. Kenneth B. Keating, "Code for Congressional Inquiries," *New York Times Magazine*, April 5, 1953, p. 10.

bility between congressional committees. Although chairmen are usually jealous of the prerogatives of their committees, they may often be reluctant to criticize another committee which begins an investigation touching on its field of competence. The initiation of an investigation by the second committee may pose particular problems, since its staff may not be be qualified to judge issues belonging primarily to the first. At least during the early 1950's and especially in terms of Asian policy, the Senate Internal Security Subcommittee served in effect as a second Foreign Relations Committee in the sense that it served as a means by which views about China policy opposed by the Foreign Relations Committee as a whole could be disseminated to the public under congressional imprimatur.

As previously noted, it would be unfair to single out the McCarran Committee for conspicuous abuse of Congressional investigatory standards. A study of the House Un-American Activities Committee (HUAC) has revealed similar criticisms of committee procedures. As Robert Carr points out, HUAC's staff was ill qualified for its multifold tasks. In addition, HUAC often disregarded time factors in assessing Communist ties of an organization and was often "content to put the finger on Communists or fellow travelers while making little or no attempt to demonstrate that they have engaged in any acts of a subversive character."[2]

Ralph Huitt's study of the Senate Banking and Finance Committee also suggests that congressional investigations are not essentially efforts at fact finding or endeavors to locate and protect the general interest. Rather, the public hearings are struggles between competing groups. Huitt found that members of the Banking and Finance Committee were seldom swayed by factual presentations at the hearings. On the whole, they merely accepted data which supported their case and rejected documentation which might buttress a contrary view.[3] Clearly, the senators on the McCarran Committee acted in a similar fashion.

2. Robert K. Carr, *The House Committee on Un-American Activities, 1945-1950*, pp. 45, 251, 454.

3. Ralph K. Huitt, "The Congressional Committee: A Case Study," *American Political Science Review*, 48 (June 1954), 354-65.

In one vitally important way, however, the McCarran Committee differed from Huitt's description of a congressional investigatory committee. In terms of its inquiry on the IPR, the committee was of one mind. Thus, the only "struggles" in the IPR investigation were contained in a one-sided contest between the senators and the representatives of the institute. Unanimity on the committee was an important factor, since it allowed the committee chairman and the staff to draft a skillful and superficially convincing report indicting the IPR.[4]

In retrospect, the McCarran Committee report can be seen as a skillful effort on the part of "conservatives" to harden American foreign policy; it was also an attempt to tarnish the image of "liberal" academicians by linking them with communism and pro-communism.[5] The McCarran hearings demonstrated clearly how a segment of Congress can utilize the Congressional investigatory process to bring out data supporting its own viewpoint on foreign policy and internal questions. The difficulty of accomplishing such tasks without committee unanimity can be seen by comparing the efforts of the McCarran Committee with that of Reece Committee investigation of foundations in 1954. Lacking unanimity, the "conservative" majority of the Reece Committee was unable to prevent questioning which placed the foundations in a more favorable light. In addition, the majority report was less skillfully drawn and its findings were undercut by two vigorous dissents.[6]

4. For an analysis of the McCarran Committee report, see below and also Chapter 4.

5. In a sense, the McCarran Committee report can be read as an indictment of most intellectuals then actively studying and analyzing Asian affairs, since most were members of the IPR. The committee report included the names of many individual Asian specialists, but made little effort to distinguish their efforts from those of the IPR leadership. The report often referred to an "IPR family" as the leading element in the organization but failed to say which members constituted this core. See *McCarran Report*, pp. 69-70, 85, 140, 151-59.

6. For a discussion of the Reece Committee's investigation of foundations, see pp. 115-16. The effort of the McCarran Committee to link "liberal" academicians with communism and pro-communism is found throughout the committee report, especially pp. 151-59.

COULD STANDARDIZED RULES HELP?

Complaints over excesses by congressional committees rose sharply as a result of the rash of congressional investigations in the security and loyalty field during the early 1950's. Several members of Congress then supported efforts to establish codes of procedure as a means of preventing excesses in such investigations. Representative (later Senator) Kenneth Keating of New York proposed one code which would have required a clear scope of inquiry for all hearings, defined the rights of witnesses, provided opportunities for rebuttal when persons were implicated during the hearings, and controlled the disclosure of executive session material or other unreleased matter.[7]

There seems little doubt that the adoption by Congress of such a code would help somewhat in protecting an individual's rights before congressional committees. No uniform code, however, can protect a witness or an organization from key factors such as one-sided questioning and dubious standards of judgment. Even if the McCarran Committee had scrupulously applied definite procedural safeguards, it is unlikely that its report would have dealt fairly with the IPR.[8] Thus, any fundamental changes in congressional investigations must depend on changes in Congress itself, and ultimately, in public opinion.

WHAT ARE PROPER STANDARDS?

The difficulty of preventing abuses in congressional investigations makes it imperative that the press and informed citizens make an effort to measure congressional standards of judgment against some sort of reasonable standard. While the formation of such a standard in security and loyalty investigations is hindered by the complexity of the subject, an effort should be made by examining some of the standards adopted by the McCarran Committee.

A difficult initial decision for any congressional committee

7. Keating, "Code for Congressional Inquiries," p. 45.

8. For a discussion of the McCarran Committee's treatment of the IPR, see Chapter 4 and below. For a brief comparison of McCarran Committee practices with the Ervin Committee's 1973 investigation of the Watergate incidents, see pp. 173-74.

conducting investigations in the internal security field is to answer the question: Who is a Communist? The McCarran Committee, while admitting that the answer was not easy, nevertheless listed its "broad basis" for defining the term. A "Communist" was not only a party member or one under the discipline of the party, but also a person "who has voluntarily and knowingly cooperated with Communist Party members in furtherance of Communist Party objectives." But the committee also argued that "from the standpoint of national security it should be noted that a well-intentioned but fuzzy-minded fellow traveler can be almost as dangerous as a knowing conspirator."[9] Obviously, such a definition could be used to encompass a wide variety of politically active people, including those making no conscious effort to serve the party.

On the other hand, it is clear that to define "Communists" merely in terms of party membership is inadequate. A person most valuable to communism might be one who is publicly known as a non-Communist, but who operates under party discipline for the accomplishment of party objectives. Nathaniel Weyl, a former Communist Party member and a witness at the McCarran hearings, has suggested the following definition: "So by Communist I mean somebody who was considered to be a person who could be relied upon, who was subordinate to the organization, who carried out orders and who worked for the party."[10]

Weyl's definition might be acceptable in some cases, but again is overly expansive. For example, it would likely encompass non-Communists blackmailed into espionage. Perhaps a better definition might be that a Communist is one who believes in the establishment of a Marxian socialist state, consciously accepts the discipline of a Communist party or group, and takes concrete actions at that party's direction for the achievement of its goals.[11] A person who

9. See *McCarran Report*, p. 123.
10. *McCarran Hearings*, p. 2812.
11. I have worded this definition to take account of the splits in the American Communist movement. In addition to the Soviet-oriented American Communist party, today's Communists should be defined to include the various Maoist organizations as well as underground terrorist groups such as the Weathermen.

demonstrates only the first quality (belief), can be termed an "ideological Communist." An individual who belongs to no organized group, but meets the other two criteria (belief and action) can be termed an "anarcho-Communist."

"Pro-Communist" was a designation often used by the McCarran Committee and, less frequently, by other critics of the IPR. Probably no other term has caused more confusion or mischief in written materials about the IPR case. The problem, of course, is that the term is usually not defined, and in fact, may be undefinable. What constitutes "pro-communism" in one man's mind may be seen merely as unconscious or inadvertent parallelism or poor judgment by another. For example, an analyst may reach an independent conclusion which coincides in part with the position which the Communist party or its members are taking at a given time. Although it offered no definition, the McCarran Committee employed the term "pro-Communist" to describe a person who had joined organizations or written for press services described by the committee as "Communist." No effort was made to determine whether the organization could be fairly described as Communist-controlled during the period of the individual's membership or that the individual was aware that the organization was being manipulated by Communists. Even membership on a large number of such groups does not necessarily establish a desire to assist communism. For example, the McCarran hearings produced substantial evidence showing that IPR staff member Maxwell Stewart had joined a remarkable number of groups later listed as Communist party fronts. No evidence was adduced, however, to indicate that Stewart's actions had come at party directive or were motivated by a desire to assist communism.

Even if reasonable evidence can establish that an individual is or has been a Communist, can it be inferred from such evidence that the individual must act as a Communist in all major activities? The McCarran Committee has given a positive answer in assessing Frederick Field's role in the IPR. In the words of the committee report, "Frederick Field was no less a Communist at this desk in the IPR office than when he reported to the Politburo of the American

Communist Party, or handed in his column to the *Daily Worker*."[12] Such an assumption seems logical. However, what does the record of the McCarran hearings and the IPR files have to say about Field's actions within the IPR? Certainly, it would be very difficult to use Field's concrete actions in the institute in order to establish that he was using the IPR for party objectives.[13] Field's writings for the IPR exhibit no political bias; neither is there evidence he urged that a "line" be adopted by *Far Eastern Survey*. Only in his attempt to merge the *Survey* and *Amerasia* can one infer any desire to encourage the IPR to take a more political stance.[14] Even in that case, it should be noted that Field quickly dropped his proposal after discovering opposition from important members of the Board of Trustees, despite the fact that his heavy contributions to the institute seemingly would have given him a degree of leverage, had he desired to use it. Of note also is that no IPR trustee ever accused Field of injecting Communist party views into the institute.[15]

The case of Frederick Field, while hardly conclusive, does suggest one hypothesis: there are some Communists skillful enough at compartmentalizing their lives that they are capable of operating as non-Communists in some segments of their existence. A corollary to this is that the party does not always insist that those accepting its discipline act as Communists in every field of endeavor. There is no doubt that the acceptance of such a hypothesis greatly complicates the task of any congressional committee in the internal security field. Nevertheless, it needs to be taken into account.

Even if definitions can be agreed upon, however, there

12. *McCarran Report*, p. 96.

13. The McCarran Committee report makes no such attempt but leaves the strong impression that Field *must* have undertaken party activities in the institute, since he was a Communist.

14. Former *Amerasia* editor Philip Jaffe does not recall any effort by Field to merge his journal with the *Survey* and doubts that such an effort was made (Jaffe to the author, September 15, 1970).

15. When the San Francisco and Seattle IPR leaders asked for Field's removal from the Board of Trustees in 1947, the issue was was solely his outside activities and public image, not his performance in the institute.

remains the problem of evidence. If committees intend to print testimony saying that X or Y is a Communist, what standards of evidence should be adopted? For the most part, the question involves the weight one attaches to hearsay evidence. Obviously, potentially the best evidence about secret organizations can be obtained from former members.

For the McCarran Committee, no problem existed. It considered communications among Communist party members as authoritative information, even when a witness had no direct information about an individual but merely repeated what he had heard from other party officials or received in official reports. Early in the hearings, Senator McCarran reminded his listeners that such "hearsay" evidence was admissible in courts of law when a conspiracy was proven or in the process of being established.[16]

What Senator McCarran did not reveal were the exact conditions under which hearsay evidence should be accepted, whether or not a conspiracy was involved. McKelvey cites two situations under which the normal proscriptions against such evidence are relaxed: (1) where it is rendered necessary by the difficulty of other proof and (2) where the circumstances under which hearsay data are originally communicated furnish some guaranty of their reliability, other than the mere fact of their having been made.[17] The McCarran Committee did not indicate in what fashion these criteria had been met in the IPR case, other than to repeat Louis Budenz' assertion that official instructions and conversations among Communist officials should be considered authoritative.[18]

Upon examination, it appears that the acceptance of hearsay evidence in the IPR case depends on two critical assumptions. The first is that Communists have a clear view of reality and can tell precisely who can be relied upon, or who is willing to carry out an instruction. Second, it assumes that Communists tell the truth to each other (the theory of comradely truth). Neither assumption is necessar-

16. *McCarran Hearings*, pp. 5-8.
17. John J. McKelvey, *Handbook of the Law of Evidence* (St. Paul, Minn.: West Publishing Company, 1924), p. 273.
18. See *McCarran Report*, p. 7.

ily valid. Normally, a decision to enter the weak and ineffective American Communist movement in a nation offering many political options does not suggest a profound grasp of reality or great emotional stability. In addition, participation in the Communist apparatus is not likely to improve an individual's judgment. Since the party's prospects have never been very good in America, there has been an understandable tendency for party leaders to exaggerate, both to its own membership and the public, its role in American life. This tendency toward exaggeration may have led party leaders, particularly during the 1930's and 1940's, to believe that they could "rely" on many more Americans than was actually the case. Such could be one explanation for Louis Budenz' testimony that professors Owen Lattimore and John Fairbank had been termed Communists in official party reports—assertions that have not stood up to the evidence either then or now.[19]

The idea that Communists always tell the truth to each other is also debatable. It seems obvious that both Soviet and American Communists have used the "big lie" in intraparty feuds, especially in an effort to purge challengers to party leaders. To assume that they are reliable in matters of personnel involves a great amount of faith.

19. No other witness at the McCarran hearings repeated Budenz' assertion that Fairbank was a party member. In Fairbank's case, no concrete actions were adduced by Budenz to support his charge. For an analysis of one of Budenz' major charges against Lattimore, see chapter 4.

A third case involving the ability of former Communists to distinguish Communists from non-Communists was that of IPR staff member Lawrence Rosinger. Two witnesses at the McCarran hearings (Karl Wittfogel and William Canning) testified that Rosinger was a member of a Communist study group at Columbia University in the late 1930's. Louis Budenz stated that Rosinger was a Communist on the basis of "official reports." Rosinger himself denied to William Holland that his research and writing had been based on anything other than his own study. However, at the McCarran hearings he invoked his Fifth Amendment privilege against possible self-incrimination when asked whether he had been a party member—a decision which effectively terminated a promising career in writing and research. No evidence was presented to show that any of Rosinger's writings in the IPR had been affected by political considerations or that he had performed any concrete actions at the request of the Communist party.

EX-COMMUNIST WITNESSES

Even if one could accept the assumptions of the McCarran Committee about hearsay evidence, additional questions can be raised about ex-Communist witnesses who provide such testimony. For Senator McCarran no problem existed. The loyalty of ex-Communists could be measured in large part by their willingness to give full testimony.[20] Not only were ex-Communist witnesses relieved of the necessity of answering searching questions; on the whole, their testimony was accepted without question.[21]

The problem would probably be manageable if it were confined to the highly publicized "professional informer" who is willing to perjure himself to obtain public acclaim. Harvey Matusow, whose testimony was accepted without any disclaimers by the McCarran Committee, falls into this category. Three years after the hearings, Matusow admitted that he had testified falsely before several committees, including the Internal Security Subcommittee. In particular, he branded as falsehoods his testimony before the McCarran Committee alleging that Owen Lattimore's books had been used as official Communist party guides to Asia. He also repudiated testimony claiming that IPR personnel vacancies were filled by Communists as a result of the institute's hiring agreement with the United Office and Professional Workers Association.[22]

However, the problem is more difficult than that suggested by the Matusow case. For most ex-Communists, the process of leaving the party, breaking with communism, and eventually testifying against former friends is a difficult experience. Many who join communism do so out of a desire to find an authoritative explanation for the happenings of a chaotic world. In many cases entry into the party means the adoption of a new, all-embracing belief. Thus, to break with communism can often mean the rejection of everything one has stood for during his adult life.

Few people like to lead their lives without any sense of

20. *McCarran Hearings*, p. 3.
21. See Chapter 4, especially pp. 86-87.
22. Harvey Matusow, *False Witness* (New York: Cameron and Kahn, 1955), p. 104.

direction or purpose. Thus, after a period of doubt and confusion, many ex-Communists search for new goals. The problem, of course, is whether or not these new goals enhance or damage the perception of reality which ex-Communists must convey to congressional committees.

The evidence on this score is not reassuring. Herbert Packer, in his excellent study of ex-Communist witnesses, has noted their tendency to substitute a new set of absolutes in place of communism. In addition, Packer notes, "The urge for self-vindication appears to be so strong that anyone who is not with them must necessarily be against them. This tendency is most noticeable in Budenz's case, but it affects the others as well."[23]

The proclivity of ex-Communist witnesses to regard existence as a struggle against implacable and highly dangerous foes raises a central question: in some cases, does the importance of the "struggle" overcome perception of reality to the detriment of innocent people? Freda Utley has posed the issue in its starkest form:

The Communist cancer must be cut out if we are to survive as a free nation. Perhaps in this operation some healthy tissues on the fringe of the Communist cancer will be destroyed. But we cannot afford, in this time of dire peril to the survival of western civilization, to refrain from eliminating the cancer which debilitates us because some innocents and dupes and some unprincipled careerists may be destroyed by the operation which is necessary if we are to stay the spread of the Communist disease.[24]

This is not to say that ex-Communists perjure themselves to aid the struggle against communism. But studies of ex-Communists do raise doubts as to their ability to provide Congress with accurate reflections of the Communist movement.

As for the conflicts between the testimony of Budenz and many of those he accused, Packer offers a plausible theory:

It may be that Budenz himself, as well as those who informed him, acting on the theory that those who cooperated with them in any respect were their friends in all respects, acquired a stock of

23. Herbert L. Packer, *Ex-Communist Witnesses: Four Studies in Fact Finding*, p. 225.

24. *Tydings Hearings*, p. 770.

names that jumbled inextricably all shades of conscious and unconscious temptation to shore up unclear recollection with clear
assertion, and it becomes quite plausible that many persons who
were never actually conscious collaborators in achieving Communist objectives were so labeled by Budenz.[25]

None of the foregoing should be taken to mean that the
public should disregard the testimony of ex-Communist
witnesses. When such a witness is effective in responding to
searching questions, when his testimony is corroborated
by other witnesses, and where concrete actions can be produced to buttress his charges, his statements may be very
valuable. Unfortunately, few congressional committees
have adopted reasonable standards of this type in dealing
with ex-Communists.

ROLE OF THE COURTS AND THE PRESS

Thus far this discussion has been concerned mainly with
congressional standards which may affect individual careers
or scholarly organizations. Although the Executive Branch
has generally been more careful than the Congress in formu-
lating its own standards of security and loyalty, in some
situations connected with the IPR case—in seeking a perjury
indictment of Owen Lattimore, and in challenging the IPR's
tax exemption—it adopted congressional norms.

Of course, Congress and the Executive did not have a
free path in actions affecting the IPR. Both formal and
informal factors in American politics altered the impact
of the governmental action toward the IPR. In examining
these factors, it is necessary to give particular attention to
the courts and the press.

In the development of American government, the courts
have served to balance and check the powers of the Congress
and the Executive Branch. In the IPR case, this function was
fully served. In its handling of the Lattimore perjury indictment, the court system demonstrated that its standards of
judgment were more demanding than those of the Congress
or the Executive. Although Lattimore's indictment was
dismissed on procedural grounds and on a tie vote, there
was enough challenge to congressional standards to justify

25. Packer, *Ex-Communist Witnesses*, p. 177.

confidence that the courts are unlikely to accept the frame of reference which has often been used by congressional investigators in internal security cases.

The courts' handling of the IPR tax appeal also suggests that the Judiciary will act as a check against the adoption of flimsy standards of evidence by the Congress and the Executive. In finding for the IPR, the court castigated the government for failing to bring its facts up to date—a charge that could be made with equal validity against the McCarran Committee.[26]

Impressive though their powers of checking and balancing may be, the courts' role can only be a limited one in cases similar to that of the IPR. The courts cannot prevent substantial damage to an organization's public image brought about by capricious actions of congressional investigatory bodies. As the IPR tax case illustrates, even when the courts do have jurisdiction, the nature of the American court system ensures that damages to an organization or an individual resulting from unfavorable publicity will not be quickly mitigated.[27]

A free press is often cited as a bulwark of democracy and especially in America as a check against excesses by government. A review of the press role in the IPR case suggests, however, that the American press does not necessarily fulfill its purported functions in each case.

As this study's analysis of press coverage of the IPR case has shown (see Chapter 4), the press provided a generally favorable dissemination of the charges made before the McCarran Committee. As a group, the daily press and mass-circulation journals did little to provide their readers with background on the IPR, or discuss the procedural or evidential standards of the McCarran Committee. In part, this pattern was the result of the practice of "straight"

26. See Decision of Court, United States District Court, Southern District of New York, *Institute of Pacific Relations* v. *United States*, March 31, 1960.

27. The possibility that courts may be somewhat more aggressive in checking Congressional abuses in the internal security field was suggested by a 1970 Federal District Court decision barring government distribution of a report listing "radical" campus speakers. *San Francisco Chronicle*, October 29, 1970.

reporting adopted by most American newspapers. That is, the remarks of a congressman or a witness at congressional hearings will be factually summarized without comment, even if the reporter personally believes them to be inaccurate. Under this system of journalism, the main criteria for publishing a story involve possible reader interest and the newness of the remarks. Whether or not the remarks are probably inaccurate or even patently absurd is irrelevant. In the IPR case this method of journalism produced a stream of sensational charges and countercharges out of which the confused reader apparently was expected to judge the institute for himself.

There is one significant factor which serves to correct abuses inherent in "straight" reporting. In time, the public bores of its novelties and prefers something different. By 1955, Senator Joseph McCarthy's remarks no longer received prominent play, largely because they were no longer "news."

It is obvious, however, that before boredom develops, "straight" reporting can cause significant damage to persons or organizations which need public trust in order to operate effectively. As this damage became more apparent in the early 1950's, media representatives and academic figures alike began to question the ethics of such reporting. Broadcaster Elmer Davis expressed strong criticism of the way in which the press had handled Senator McCarthy's "exposures."[28] Robert Carr, who studied press handling of investigations conducted by the House Un-American Activities Committee, complained that

> . . . even the best papers have all too frequently played up sensational witnesses, however irresponsible their testimony, have failed to report adequately the testimony of calmer witnesses or the replies of those who have been attacked, and have opened their columns too readily to the most trivial, ridiculous, or incredible musings, speculations, and predictions of committee members.[29]

Despite such qualms, the nature of the news business and especially the difficulty of determining what is "irresponsi-

28. Elmer Davis, *But We Were Born Free* (Indianapolis: Bobbs, Merrill, 1954), p. 25.

29. Carr, *The House Committee on Un-American Activities*, p. 404.

ble" testimony or a "trumped-up" incident has posed serious obstacles to the efforts of those seeking to mitigate the excesses of "straight" reporting. While the problem has been alleviated somewhat by greater use of "interpretive" reporting, the basic issues remain. The political neutrality of "straight" reporting has also become more evident with the passage of time. Whereas its excesses were of concern primarily to "liberals" and members of the left during the the 1950's, this type of journalism is now coming under increasing attack from "conservatives" and moderates, who charge that it distorts reality and gives comfort to radicals.[30]

SOME LESSONS FROM THE IPR CASE

The experience of the Institute of Pacific Relations, both in its own development and in its clash with elements of the American political system, has applications far beyond one organization or even Asian studies. The lessons of the IPR case are applicable also to many private groups.

In discussing these lessons, it is best to deal first with allegations against the IPR often raised in the press and especially by the McCarran Committee. While they are not the most significant issues raised by the IPR case, they became so in the public media as the result of America's public mood, journalistic practices, and the efforts of politicians whose real concerns were foreign policy and internal security, rather than Asian studies or the functioning of private groups in America.

The first and most important charge raised by witnesses at the McCarran hearings was that the institute was infiltrated by Communists and subject to control or manipulation by either the American Communist party or Soviet intelligence. To begin with, it should be noted that while the McCarran Committee provided a highly favorable forum for such charges, the committee's own conclusions were far less expansive. The committee claimed only that the institute had been controlled by a small core of officials and that unidentified "members" of this core were "either Communist

30. See, for example, Daniel P. Moynihan, "The Presidency and the Press," *National Observer*, March 29, 1971.

or pro-Communist." It further alleged that both the American Communist party and Soviet officials had considered the IPR "as an instrument of Communist policy, propaganda and military intelligence."[31]

There is little doubt that a relatively small number of people played a predominant role in the IPR. They were not always the same people, however, nor were they subject to central direction. Edward Carter may have hoped for stronger AIPR coverage of controversial political questions in East Asia. He did not get it from the *Far Eastern Survey*, however, as long as Russell Shiman was its editor. Neither can it be said that Carter or any group of IPR leaders had decisive say over the institute's main product, book-length research about Asia.

Whether or not members of the IPR leadership core were Communist or pro-Communist depends on who one includes as IPR leaders and how "Communist" and "pro-Communist" are defined. If the terms are defined in the manner earlier suggested in this chapter, and if the IPR core is defined to include only key officials (founders, secretaries-general, key trustees, editors of journals, and veteran staff members), the only influential leader justifying a "Communist" label is Frederick Field. Even in Field's case, however, evidence introduced at the McCarran hearings did not establish that he had taken concrete actions within the IPR at the party's request.

Whether or not Communist party leaders regarded the IPR as an instrument of party policy or propaganda is not easy to say. It does seem clear that some former Communists, and especially Louis Budenz, had obtained that impression. The main issue, however, is not what Communists may have thought, but whether or not they were able to carry out concrete programs through the IPR. Unfortunately, the McCarran hearings offer very little evidence on this point. The most detailed charge offered to the McCarran Committee was Louis Budenz' assertion that the Communists attempted to put across the view that the Chinese Communists were merely agrarian radicals. Budenz asserted that this program eventually found fruition in T. A. Bisson's article on "demo-

31. *McCarran Report*, pp. 223-26.

cratic" and "feudal" China in the *Far Eastern Survey*.[32]
At the Tydings hearings Budenz implied that Lattimore had
a part in this campaign.[33] However, he failed to explain
why *Pacific Affairs* under Lattimore's editorship gave
rather scant attention to the Chinese Communists and failed
to promote an "agrarian radical" image for the Chinese
Communists; nor did he make clear why Lattimore was
responsible for the appearance of an article in a journal
he did not then edit.

The McCarran Committee's attempt to link the IPR with
Soviet propaganda and intelligence efforts is plausible only
if one is willing to accept on faith the testimony of former
Soviet officials who admittedly were not closely involved in
dealings with the IPR. The committee could have demonstrated convincingly that institute officials, especially
Edward Carter and Owen Lattimore, were exceedingly
favorable to the USSR and offered the Soviets a golden
opportunity to participate heavily in the IPR. Had they
chosen to do so, it is quite conceivable that heavy opposition
to Carter's leadership within the IPR might have developed
much earlier than it did. For their own reasons, however,
the Soviets did not respond to Carter's efforts.

Probably the one allegation of the McCarran Committee
most unfair to an individual was the charge that Owen
Lattimore had been a "conscious articulate instrument of
the Soviet conspiracy."[34] Several criticisms can be made of
Lattimore—namely, that he was at times not a neutral
editor of *Pacific Affairs,* that he offered bad advice on the
Inquiry Project, that his views of Soviet domestic and foreign
policy were often inaccurate, that his judgments of the views
of Asian "peoples" were often far too sweeping, and that
he did little to disabuse the public of the idea that he had
all the answers to the problems of American policy in Asia.
These are factors the public or members of the Asian studies
field ought to consider in evaluating a man's general reliability or his qualifications to edit a major journal in the field.
But they hardly justify the extreme conclusion of the

32. See *McCarran Hearings*, pp. 529-30.
33. *Tydings Hearings*, p. 492.
34. *McCarran Report*, p. 224.

McCarran Committee. In fact, it is difficult to conclude that Owen Lattimore was the conscious articulate instrument of anything but his own unusual and unorthodox background and thinking.

Summing up its case against the IPR, the McCarran Committee concluded that "the net effect of IPR activities on United States public opinion has been such as to serve international Communist interests and to affect adversely the interests of the United States."[35] There are several problems in such an assertion. To begin with, it is very difficult even to approximate the IPR's total impact without making some effort to examine its major output—booklength research. Although the committee could have requested assistance from specialists in the Library of Congress or obtained outside consultants to examine the results of IPR research, there is no evidence that it did so. In addition, the committee's report did not define the meaning of either "international Communist interest" or "American interests."

MAJOR ISSUES UNNOTED AND UNRESOLVED

In treating the IPR case as a security issue, the McCarran Committee report largely ignored many important issues in the rise and fall of the Institute of Pacific Relations. The press, by emphasizing the charges of the ex-Communists and the countercharges of those accused of Communist ties, also contributed to the impression that the major issues of the IPR case involved national security. As the preceding sections have made clear, such a conclusion can only be sustained with a very broad definition of national security and a willingness to accept with few questions the testimony of the ex-Communist witnesses.

If national security is not the main question, what issues lie at the heart of the IPR case? Several require mention; some relate in whole or part to the unusual nature of the IPR and its leadership; others are more general and have applications for Asian studies and all private groups. At their core these issues relate to scholarly and philosophical issues rather than national security.

35. Ibid., p. 225.

The desirability of clarity in the goals of an organization is one vital issue emerging from the IPR case. While the IPR constitution stated that the institute had been formed to "study the conditions of the Pacific peoples with a view to the improvement of their mutual relations," considerable confusion existed on just what this meant and what was entailed in order to achieve it. Was the institute primarily an organization set up to arrange for exchanges of views between Westerners and Asians? Should research be its primary goal and, if so, what type of research? Should IPR publications involve themselves in matters of current dispute in East Asian politics? All of these questions received implicit answers in the course of the history of the IPR. Unfortunately, they were seldom posed in clear-cut fashion for decision by the Pacific Council, the trustees of the American IPR, or the membership. Had the issues been discussed clearly at an early date, it might have been more evident from the outset that certain types of research would not necessarily be compatible with the goal of bringing together private citizens from Asia and the West.

A second fundamental issue in the development of the IPR concerns the nature of leadership in private organizations. Essentially this involves the relationship between policy-making organs and the staff. In the case of the IPR, and especially the International IPR, problems resulted when duly constituted executive organs failed to make policy. This pattern was highlighted by the failure of the Pacific Council in 1936 to provide firm guidelines for the editing of *Pacific Affairs,* even when they were sought by Owen Lattimore. Inevitably, the staff was forced to improvise without clear guidance—a situation which usually invites trouble unless a staff is exemplary in its conduct and clearly representative of the membership.

Of course, the IPR's unique international structure hindered effective policy-making by executive organs. The diverse international composition of the Pacific Council effectively prevented clear-cut decisions. Even within the American Council, it was not always easy to ensure the attendance of West Coast trustees. This was unfortunate, since those trustees were generally more sympathetic than

East Coast representatives to membership complaints about the leadership in New York.

Even if the structure of the IPR foisted a great deal of responsibility on the staff, it is nevertheless necessary to ask how this task was carried out by the IPR leadership, and especially by Edward Carter. In one sense, Carter must be given a good deal of credit. Without his zeal in organizing national councils, the institute's name would not have become known in so many lands. Without his vigor and skill in approaching foundations in New York, IPR research would never have reached such high levels. Carter's drive and zeal, however, were often not matched by adequate concern for the consequences of new programs for the ultimate health of the IPR. Neither did he always make an adequate effort to get the membership on board before embarking on new programs. Tact and patience in implementing programs were not among his assets. As a result, when disputes about his leadership finally broke into the open in 1947, they involved demands from West Coast chapters that he end his leadership role in the IPR.

Aside from questions of executive authority, the IPR case also illustrates another problem of leadership in private groups: the relationship between a leader's official duties and his private actions. The experiences of the Institute of Pacific Relations demonstrate clearly the desirability of a sharp separation between official and nonofficial acts. By failing to make this separation in several instances involving foreign policy issues, Edward Carter left the IPR open to charges of lobbying.

Problems of regionalism in American private groups constitute a third fundamental issue illustrated by the IPR case. There is little doubt that regionalism in the American IPR was accentuated by personality conflicts and differing visions about the nature of the institute. However, problems of regionalism in the IPR were in part those which must be faced by any American private group which seeks to operate on a national scale and encourages the formation of strong local or regional units. To some extent, leaders of private organizations must face problems similar to American political leaders in devising programs which not only seem sensible to a group's national leadership but also are acceptable to widely divergent regional constituencies. This problem was intensified in the case of the IPR by the location of institute headquarters in New York. New York was a logical choice in view of its accessibility to foundations and availability of qualified personnel. The shift of IPR headquarters from Hawaii to New York was not an unqualified advantage, however, since the political atmosphere of New York during the 1930's and 1940's probably insulated the IPR leadership from the concerns of its more "conservative" members and leaders on the West Coast.

A fourth lesson resulting from the IPR experience is the difficulty of maintaining a private organization which sponsors research on matters involving political controversy. In attempting to actualize such a difficult experiment, the IPR found its members constantly at odds about the propriety of certain types of research. The Japanese were never happy with institute research on the Sino-Japanese War; English delegates were often critical of institute treatment of British colonialism; Chinese delegates occasionally protested coverage on Nationalist China; and Soviet officials demonstrated a high degree of sensitivity to anything even remotely critical of the USSR. No satisfactory method was found to carry out the IPR's diverse objectives in the face of such contradictory advice.

A fifth question raised by the IPR case concerns the relationship between creativity and political safety in American private groups. As this study has demonstrated, Edward Carter and other IPR leaders placed few restrictions on the activities of staff members, even when failure to do so created difficulties with elements in the institute. Neither did IPR leaders conduct political background checks on prospective employees or writers for institute publications. The absence of such restrictions was an important element in recruiting a dedicated staff with high morale. Despite the low pay offered staff members, the IPR became an attractive place to work because of its atmosphere for creativity and close staff camaraderie.[36]

36. Philip Lilienthal, former editor of *Pacific Affairs*, now recalls his IPR days as among the most exciting and stimulating of his life (Lilienthal, personal interview, July 8, 1970).

Ultimately, however, a heavy price was paid for such freedom. The McCarran Committee, while failing to prove that Communists used the IPR for party purposes, was able to damage the institute's image by establishing that Communists such as Frederick Field, Chi Chao-ting, James Allen, and "Asiaticus" had either been employed by the IPR or had contributed to its publications. Even before the IPR's collision with the McCarran Committee, allegations of communism had played a role in local pressures in San Francisco and Seattle which encouraged local institute leaders to believe they should remove their groups from the IPR.

Finally, the IPR case illustrates the limitations inherent in all social science research, and especially research which attempts to clarify items of immediate interest. In retrospect, the coverage of such areas as Soviet foreign policy and the Chinese Communist movement in *Pacific Affairs* and *Far Eastern Survey* was shallow and lacking in perception. To those engaged in research, that conclusion may not be very surprising in view of the lack of good source materials at the time, the scarcity of trained personnel, the fluidity of the situation, and the problem of human frailty. Today, improvements in training and source materials, plus the hindsight of earlier experiences, have increased the chances for more accurate and perceptive analysis of such issues. Nevertheless, human limitations and the inherent problems of analysis remain—factors which researchers should candidly admit to themselves and especially to the public.

In the final analysis, the real questions of the Institute of Pacific Relations do not involve security or loyalty. They involve the very essence of scholarship: the ability to deal fairly with factual data; the willingness to examine all facts and interpretations even when they are counter to one's past interpretations; and most important, the willingness to alter one's position upon the discovery of new facts and the candor to admit that one has altered his view. Robert North, an Asian scholar, once put it this way:

The responsibility of the scholar and writer, it seems to me, is neither simply to present the Soviet view, or any other view, without comment; nor to decide hastily that the Moscow trials are democratic (or undemocratic). It is not for either of these relatively uncomplicated tasks that he has subjected himself to years of specialized study and discipline. Rather, he is supposed carefully to check and sift and weigh and analyze the evidence in a soul-wracking search for the truth. Anything less is a prostitution of his profession.[37]

Of course, to define a standard is one thing, to assess its operation in a particular case quite another. Probably every Asian scholar at some time has failed to live up to the high standard offered by North; it is also necessary to bear in mind a warning from Paul Linebarger, who has asked: "Is there not, however, a real possibility that facts of this kind which we have been seeking very soon exhaust their usefulness and that problems of ethical judgment, of personal philosophy, color each individual's interpretation of the China scene?"[38] It would be impossible, and in fact undesirable, to eliminate the personal factor cited by Linebarger. But scholars do have the responsibility of making their judgments as clearly as possible, fairly summarizing opposing views, and letting their readers know where they can find contrary interpretations.

By what process can the high standards previously mentioned be maintained? How can the public be convinced of the integrity of Asian scholars? In the end, only the members of the field can perform that task properly. Only vigorous criticism by their peers can ensure that standards are met, that prejudice or special pleading is exposed, factual data verified, and interpretations substantiated or challenged. No higher court can render such judgments.[39]

Nevertheless, it should be admitted that courts of scholarly peers do not always function to perfection. In the case of IPR publications, critical exchanges among scholars were relatively few. When T. A. Bisson used the terms "democratic" and "feudal" to describe Communist- and Nationalist-controlled areas of China during 1943, only a Chinese National-

---

37. North to William L. Holland, July 3, 1952, Columbia Files.

38. Paul M. A. Linebarger, "Outside Pressures on China, 1945-1950," *Annals of the American Academy of Political and Social Science,* 277 (September 1951): 177.

39. See Glenn R. Morrow, "Academic Freedom," *AAUP Bulletin,* 40 (Winter 1954-55): 532.

ist official replied in print. When *Far Eastern Survey* editor Laurence Salisbury implied that the Chinese Communists might not be true Communists, his view went unchallenged. When *Pacific Affairs* published Harriet Moore's uncritical views on Soviet foreign policy, no dissents were recorded As previously mentioned, lack of vigorous criticism in the field resulted in part from limitations in training and materials. It also resulted, in the case of the IPR, from excessive politeness on the part of Asian scholars toward one another's work.

A related question concerns the attitude which the field and the public should adopt toward writings by nonscholars or members of the field who do not consistently demonstrate strict standards of research or interpretation. An example might be the writing of Edgar Snow about China. Snow did not claim scholarly knowledge about China. He attempted to convey the impressions of a journalist with unique Western access to the Chinese Communist leadership. In books and articles over the years, Snow conveyed a good deal of data about the attitudes of Chinese leaders. On the other hand, he often failed to deal with the more negative phenomena in Chinese communism, unless the Chinese leaders themselves were willing to concede such shortcomings.

How should the field or the public evaluate work by authors such as Snow? The McCarran Committee had no difficulty answering that question. Snow was labelled "pro-Communist," on the grounds that he had participated in organizations claimed to be Communist fronts.[40] Although the committee did not say so directly, it is reasonable to assume that Snow was one of the authors that Senator McCarran and his colleagues had in mind when they referred to a "net pro-Communist effect" from IPR publications.[41] A second approach might be simply to dismiss all of Snow's writings as valueless on the grounds that they have been "unscholarly."

40. *McCarran Report*, p. 100.
41. Ibid., p. 95. It should be made clear that whatever the impression left by the McCarran Committee report, Snow was not active in the IPR.

There seems no sound reason to adopt either of these approaches. The first places undue faith in the testimony of ex-Communists and ignores the motivation of individuals joining such groups. The second is an all-or-nothing type of position which disregards the potential contributions of diverse personalities. What is needed is an approach which utilizes the strengths of writers like Snow while clarifying obvious weaknesses. In Snow's writing a reader could expect to find a relatively authoritative exposition of the views of Chinese Communist leaders as well as eye-witness descriptions of life in various parts of China. Probably less valuable would be Snow's overall interpretation of events in China and his views on Sino-United States relations. When read alone, Snow's works leave many gaps. But when read in conjunction with other materials, they provide valuable data.

For the public, of course, the problem is more difficult. Without adequate background, a general reader might have little with which to compare interpretations from a single source. It is in situations like these that members of a scholarly field can be of assistance to the general public. To a greater extent than they have previously, they ought to convey to the public the degree of diversity which exists among writers dealing with East Asia and the reasons for such diversity. In addition, frank admissions about the human frailties of scholars and the difficulties of analysis should help to undercut future claims that the public was misled by "so-called scholars."

THE ARGUMENT FOR OUTSIDE INTERVENTION CONSIDERED

In practice the Asian studies field in America has not always been left alone to work out its own academic controversies or even the organization of its field. Beginning with Alfred Kohlberg's charges against the IPR in 1944, Senator McCarthy's broadside against Owen Lattimore in 1950, and culminating with the McCarran Committee investigation of the IPR in 1951-52, nonacademic forces impinged on the Asian studies field.

It is important to examine the philosophical justification for political movements which have affected Asian studies. William Buckley, in his defense of the McCarthy movement, has offered an important point of view. Writing in 1954, he defined the McCarthy movement as a campaign by which Americans rallied around an orthodoxy which had the exclusion of communism as its chief characteristic. The only conformity at issue, Buckley insisted, was one which excluded Communists from the centers of American life. He derided the idea that American intellectuals were operating under a reign of terror, or that the "growing firmness" in America would also be felt by "any deviate from the line laid down at the last assembly of the National Association of Manufacturers. . . ."[42]

There are several problems with Buckley's analysis which are apparent from the IPR case. In the first place, the definition of the word, "Communist," by the McCarran Committee was so broad as to include many individuals having no proven identity of purpose with the Communist party. Buckley admitted that the McCarthy movement may have involved some imperfect sanctions against dissidents, but nevertheless gave his approval to the movement as a whole.[43] Second, the McCarran Committee did not confine its fire to Communist party members but charged numerous scholars with an undefined "pro-communism." Buckley himself exhibits this tendency by categorizing Owen Lattimore as a "fellow-traveler."[44]

In addition, the McCarran Committee investigation of the IPR introduced added strains into Asian studies by in effect inviting some members of the field to testify against others. Although the McCarran Committee did not manufacture disputes among Asian specialists, it aided the presentation of disagreements in a form which intensified personal animosities in the field.

In terms of the IPR case, probably the most serious effect of the efforts of Alfred Kohlberg, Senator McCarthy, and the McCarran Committee was to transform legitimate issues of interpretation of events in East Asia and the organization of Asian studies into questions of loyalty and security. In the process, the original issues were obscured and their

42. William F. Buckley, Jr., and L. Brent Bozell, *McCarthy and His His Enemies*, (Chicago: Regnery, 1954), pp. 311-12.
43. Ibid., p. 331.
44. Ibid., pp. 311-12.

solution made more difficult. Far from aiding balance and objectivity in IPR publications, Kohlberg's charges merely added to the problems of institute members seeking change in the policies of the leadership in New York. In a similar fashion, the treatment of the IPR by the McCarran Committee encouraged members of the Asian studies field to rise to the defense of the institute rather than to engage in a careful analysis of the strengths and weaknesses of the IPR.

In retrospect it seems clear that Buckley was accurate in asserting that intellectuals in America did not operate under a reign of terror during the early 1950's. But just as clearly, intellectual leaders at the time *believed* that significant threats existed to academic freedom. Thus, a major drawback of the McCarthy movement of the early 1950's was the large diversion of time and energy of intellectuals from more productive duties such as teaching or research.[45]

Movements such as those of the early 1950's have also been justified on the grounds that they promote a higher degree of security and loyalty in government. In the area of document security, some initial improvements probably took place in response to congressional pressures to tighten the lax procedures revealed in the *Amerasia* case. Tighter procedural requirements, however, have not prevented the unauthorized disclosure of even top-secret government documents, as shown by the publication of the Pentagon Papers.

In terms of loyalty, the results of such movements are even

45. This observation can also be applied to the impact of America's participation in Vietnam on Asian scholars.

In terms of the functioning of government, the impact of the McCarthy movement was undoubtedly much greater. The State Department's China service lost several of its leading figures as a result of the government's preoccupation with security and loyalty during the early fifties. It should be noted that none of the Foreign Service China specialists resigned or was removed as a result of evidence that he had been disloyal to the nation. In each case, sloppy security practices or poor judgment was given as the reason for removal, despite the fact that government security practices in general during the 1930's and 1940's were very lax. The sanctions on security grounds were also discriminatory, since they singled out Foreign Service officers who had indicated doubts about the viability of the Chinese Nationalists and the wisdom of all-out American support for President Chiang.

more dubious. As Morton Grodzins has pointed out, men are likely to be most loyal when their jobs and careers are secure, their relations with colleagues and friends amiable, and their relationships to the general community are not strained. An overemphasis on investigations and background checks is thus likely to be counterproductive to loyalty.[46]

WHERE ARE WE NOW?

Thus far this study has examined the controversies surrounding the Institute of Pacific Relations primarily in terms of the context of the 1930's, the 1940's, and the 1950's. But many of the issues raised in the IPR case—the standards and practices of congressional investigating committees, the relations between intellectuals and government officials, and United States views on Asia generally—have a continuing relevance for the 1970's. It is therefore helpful to conclude by sketching in a more current perspective.

The 1973 Senate hearings into the Watergate incidents, taking place as this book went to press, give some indication of current congressional standards with regard to investigatory committees. In several ways, the Ervin Committee is a good deal fairer to its witnesses than was the McCarran Committee: witnesses are usually not badgered in making answers and are allowed to consult counsel before answering questions; they are allowed to read even lengthy statements into the record without harassment; the open display of bias by Ervin Committee members is also much less in comparison to those on the McCarran Committee; in addition, a better range of questions are asked by members of the Ervin Committee, since the members are not all of one mind about the involvement of various individuals in the Watergate affair.

However, the possibility that the Watergate hearings may unfairly damage the reputations of individuals cannot be denied. Intensive television and radio coverage of the hearings heightens this possibility. In addition, of course, the Ervin hearings may have the undesirable feature of preventing successful prosecution of those accused of criminal action,

46. Morton Grodzins, *The Loyal and the Disloyal: Social Boundaries of Patriotism and Treason* (Chicago: University of Chicago Press, 1956), p. 236.

since widespread publicity of the charges may make it impossible for any potential defendant to receive a fair trial.

Clearly by 1973 the impact of political forces in Congress on Asian studies had sharply declined from its peak in the 1950's.[47] No longer were congressional loyalty-security hearings a matter of great current interest. Even the Senate Internal Security Subcommittee, the investigator of the IPR, had shown signs of mellowing. The House Committee on Internal Security, the successor to the Un-American Activities Committee, was a pale shadow of its controversial predecessor. In California, the state Senate had abolished its own Un-American Activities Committee.

Only occasionally, and without fanfare, did the conspiracy theory of American foreign policy re-emerge for public consumption. At hearings on China policy before the Senate Foreign Relations Committee in 1966, Professor David Rowe diverged sharply from his colleagues by testifying that "pro-Red China" people in America were "much more dangerous than the Southeast Asian Communists" because they might help bring about a frame of mind which would weaken America's will to assist in defense against Communist aggression.[48] In 1970, the Senate Internal Security Subcommittee gave further publicity to an extension of the conspiracy theory as applied to America's Asian policy. In a long introduction to the committee's release of documents from the *Amerasia* case, Professor Anthony Kubek stated the thesis clearly:

The fall of the Chinese mainland to Communism has since come to be regarded throughout the free world as the greatest single tragedy of modern times. The terrible wars in Korea and Vietnam have resulted directly from the Communist seizure of the Asiatic heart-

47. The extent to which the legacy of congressional involvement in America's Asian policies continued to affect presidential war policies was less clear. Certainly the legacy of the early 1950's was one factor in the complex process leading to U.S. intervention in Indochina. See *Newsweek*, July 12, 1971, p. 22.

48. U.S., Congress, Senate, Committee on Foreign Relations, *Hearings on U.S. Policy with Respect to Mainland China*, 89th Cong., 2d sess., 1966, pp. 525-537. Rowe's assertion that the hearings might assist the interests of the Chinese Communists was sharply disputed by Senator George Aiken, the committee's ranking Republican. See ibid., pp. 532-33.

land, and all the brewing difficulties elsewhere in the Far East over the past two decades have had the cancer of China at their root.[49]

Books by Kubek and John Stormer also attempted to keep the conspiracy theory alive.[50] None of these efforts, however, received large public notice. Probably of greater significance were works by two former State Department officials who had been charged with disloyalty during the McCarthy era.[51]

By 1973, the major question was whether the relative lack of political phenomena similar to those of the early 1950's amounted to only a temporary lull or indicated that a new McCarthy movement was unlikely to recur. On the one hand, such social science research as was available indicated that the American public, despite its fluctuating support for Senator McCarthy during the early 1950's, had not exhibited convincing signs of anxiety over the issues McCarthy had raised.[52] Such research was consistent with the viewpoint of historian Richard Hofstadter, who has noted that most Americans are neither prointellectual nor anti-intellectual, but nonintellectual.[53]

Despite such evidence of the lack of a strong base for a McCarthyist revival, events of the 1960's and early 1970's demonstrated that major American politicians had not given up the idea that fears of change on the part of the voters can be tapped for political benefit, or at least that sentiments of that type needed to be placated. In the past decade the country

49. See U.S., Congress, Senate, Committee on the Judiciary, Subcommittee on Internal Security, *The Amerasia Papers: A Clue to the Catastrophe of China*, 91st Cong., 1st sess., 1970, p. 1.

50. See Anthony Kubek, *How the Far East Was Lost: American Policy and the Creation of Communist China, 1941-1949* (Chicago: Regnery, 1963); and John Stormer, *None Dare Call It Treason* (Florissant, Mo.: Liberty Bell Press, 1964).

51. See John S. Service, *The Amerasia Papers: Some Problems in the History of U.S.-China Relations* (Berkeley: Center for Chinese Studies, University of California, 1971); and John Paton Davies, *Dragon By the Tail: American, British, Japanese Encounters with China and One Another* (New York: Norton, 1972).

52. Samuel A. Stouffer, *Communism, Conformity, and Civil Liberties* (Garden City, N.Y.: Doubleday, 1955), p. 59.

53. Richard Hofstadter, *Anti-Intellectualism in American Life* (New York: Alfred A. Knopf, 1963), p. 19.

had witnessed the Goldwater campaign, with its stress on "victory" in foreign policy and a defense of "extremism" in the defense of "liberty"; the Wallace movement, with its undisguised anti-intellectual ridicule of the "pointy-heads"; and finally, Vice President Agnew's efforts to link his party's opponents with radicalism at home and defeatism abroad. None of these efforts had been notably successful, but the persistence of such movements suggested that major American politicians continued to believe that political positions and tactics reminiscent of the early 1950's occasionally still had a place in the politics of the 1970's. In themselves, such efforts did not presage a return to the climate of the early fifties. Other factors, such as foreign policy reverses, security scandals, or other shocks to the political system would likely be required to bring that about. Nevertheless, the experience of the 1960's suggested that as in the 1950's, major American political forces might temporarily cooperate with or seek to placate new movements similar to those of Joseph McCarthy.

Just as the political climate affecting Asian studies had changed since the 1950's, the field itself had undergone changes in mood. By the early 1960's, time had healed much of the bitterness among Asian scholars that had emerged from the congressional investigations a decade earlier. For a short moment it appeared that the field might be able to enter a more relaxed era in which it faced fewer pressures from political forces or personal disputes.

Such hopes were gradually dissipated in the reaction of both students and professors to America's growing military involvement in Indochina and the nation's difficulties in solving its internal problems. Once again, foreign policy questions had created new divisions between Asian specialists and government. The difficulties for Asian specialists increased as the Vietnam War intensified and protests through regular channels failed to halt America's involvement.

Should they speak out? In what form? Should they participate in political movements related to the war? Should they urge their professional groups to take a stand? What obligations did they have as Asian specialists? All of these were questions faced in somewhat different form by their predecessors during the thirties and forties. Now they were posed again in even more pressing form.

Just as important developments in Asia had affected America's Asian studies in earlier decades, they now deeply affected the field as well as intellectuals generally. But this time it was apparent that the impact would be different. In Asian studies the older animosities between "conservatives" and "liberals" in the field were often no longer the key issue; instead both groups found themselves increasingly under attack from leftist students claiming that Asian scholars should take not only a political stand on the war but also should actively work for fundamental changes in the field and society.[54] As the 1970's began, it had become increasingly evident that intolerance and intimidation on campus on the part of the New Left posed new and difficult problems for academic freedom generally and especially for Asian studies—problems which rivaled any potential threats from political forces.[55]

In 1973, another unresolved issue of the IPR case had resurfaced—the question of interpretation of the Chinese Communist movement. From the viewpoint of the sixties, it appeared that the primary problems of giving an accurate impression of Chinese communism during earlier times had involved issues such as a writer's degree of preparation in China and especially his or her understanding of Marxist-Leninist theory and practice. An additional problem seemed to be the fact that many journalists of the 1930's and 1940's quite understandably found the vitality of the Communist areas of China a vivid comparison with the lethargy, corruption, and general malaise of wartime Nationalist China.

After the return of American journalists to China in 1972, however, it was apparent that the problems of providing

54. These trends were evident at the April 1970 meeting of the Concerned Asian Scholars. At one session, Professor Fairbank, who had supported the creation of CCAS, found himself under strong criticism from other panelists, including one of his own students.

55. In answering a letter from a Harvard student, sociologist David Riesman noted that intimidation was not a one-way street. He believed that in the late 1960's it was his more conservative undergraduates who felt intimidated by the atmosphere at Harvard and Radcliffe. See *Bulletin of Concerned Asian Scholars*, 1 (October 1968): 8.

accurate and balanced interpretations of Chinese communism were more complex. By 1973, even hard-nosed American journalistic opponents of Chinese communism seemed deeply affected by visits to the People's Republic. That the American people were once again treated to a series of glowing accounts of life in China made it clear that the vigor of Chinese communism continued to impress foreign reporters. Once again, however, it was very difficult from journalistic accounts to obtain an accurate impression of the means by which improvements in material well-being had been achieved.

The role of the party, revolutionary committees, and small groups in motivating the behavior of individuals was often slighted in comparison with accounts of the more obvious and visual improvements in Chinese life since 1949. Thus, by 1973 it seemed no easier to obtain a well-rounded account of Chinese communism than in the 1930's or 1940's.

Whatever the outcome of these problems, it was apparent that many of the issues faced by the Institute of Pacific Relations were not dead, but present again in new garb. Certainly, the achievements of the IPR had been many. Hopefully, the lessons of its experience would not be lost for those Americans, young and old alike, who continued to find the study of modern Asia a fascinating and engrossing experience.

Sources Consulted

BOOKS

Almond, Gabriel A. *The American People and Foreign Policy.* New York: Harcourt, Brace, 1950.

Anderson, Jack, and Ronald May. *McCarthy: The Man, the Senator, the "Ism."* Boston: Beacon Press, 1952.

Andrews, Bert. *Washington Witch Hunt.* New York: Random House, 1948.

Barth, Alan. *Government by Investigation.* New York: Viking Press, 1955.

Bell, Daniel, ed. *The Radical Right.* Garden City, N.J.: Doubleday, 1963.

Boas, George, and Harvey Wheeler, eds. *Lattimore the Scholar.* Baltimore, Md.: 1953.

Boorman, Howard L., ed. *Moscow-Peking Axis: Strengths and Strains.* New York: Harper, 1957.

Borg, Dorothy. *Historians and American Far Eastern Policy.* New York: Columbia University Press, 1966.

Buckley, William F., Jr. *God and Man at Yale: The Superstitions of "Academic Freedom."* Chicago: Regnery, 1951.

———, and L. Brent Bozell. *McCarthy and His Enemies.* Chicago: Regnery, 1954.

Budenz, Louis F. *The Cry Is Peace.* Chicago: Regnery, 1952.

———. *Men without Faces.* New York: Harper, 1950.

———. *The Techniques of Communism.* Chicago: Regnery, 1954.

———. *This Is My Story.* New York: Whittlesey, 1947.

Carr, Robert K. *The House Un-American Activities Committee.* Ithaca, N.Y.: Cornell University Press, 1952.

Chambers, Whittaker. *Witness*. New York: Random House, 1952.

The China White Paper (1949). Stanford, Calif.: Stanford University Press, 1967.

Commager, Henry Steele. *Freedom and Order*. New York: George Braziller, 1966.

———. *Freedom, Loyalty, Dissent*. New York: Oxford University Press, 1954.

Dallin, David. *Soviet Espionage*. New Haven, Conn.: Yale University Press, 1955.

Davies, John Paton. *Dragon By the Tail: American, British, Japanese Encounters with China and One Another*. New York: Norton, 1972.

Davis, Elmer. *But We Were Born Free*. Indianapolis: Bobbs-Merrill, 1954.

Davis, John Merle. *An Autobiography*. Kyo Bun Kwan, undated.

Draper, Theodore. *The Roots of American Communism*. New York: Viking Press, 1957.

Epstein, Israel. *The Unfinished Revolution in China*. Boston: Little, Brown, and Co., 1947.

Feis, Herbert. *The China Tangle*. Princeton, N.J.: Princeton University Press, 1953.

Flynn, John Thomas. *The Lattimore Story*. New York: Devin-Adair, 1953.

Goldman, Eric F. *The Crucial Decade*. New York: Alfred A. Knopf, 1956.

Grodzins, Morton. *The Loyal and the Disloyal: Social Boundaries of Patriotism and Treason*. Chicago: University of Chicago Press, 1956.

Hofstadter, Richard. *Anti-intellectualism in American Life*. New York: Alfred A. Knopf, 1963.

———. *The Paranoid Style in American Politics*. New York: Alfred A. Knopf, 1965.

Horn, Robert A. *Groups and the Constitution*. Stanford, Calif.: Stanford University Press, 1956.

Howe, Irving. *The American Communist Party: A Critical History, 1919-1957*. Boston: Beacon Press, 1957.

Jensen, Oliver, ed. *America and Russia*. New York: Simon and Schuster, 1963.

Kahin, George McTurnan, and John W. Lewis. *The United States in Vietnam*. New York: Dial Press, 1967.

Keeley, Joseph. *The China Lobby Man*. New Rochelle, N.Y.: Arlington House, 1969.

Kirwin, Harry W. *The Inevitable Success: Herbert R. O'Conor*. Westminster, Md.: Newman Press, 1962.

Koen, Ross Y. *The China Lobby in American Politics.* New York: Macmillan, 1960.

Kubek, Anthony. *How the Far East Was Lost: American Policy and the Creation of Communist China, 1941-1949.* Chicago: Regnery, 1963.

Lasswell, Harold. *National Security and Individual Freedom.* New York: McGraw-Hill, 1950.

Latham, Earl. *The Communist Controversy in Washington: From the New Deal to McCarthy.* Cambridge, Mass.: Harvard University Press, 1966.

Lattimore, Owen. *Ordeal by Slander.* Boston: Little, Brown, 1950.

Lazarfield, Paul F., and Wagner Thielens, Jr. *The Academic Mind.* Glencoe, Ill.: Free Press, 1958.

MacIver, Robert M. *Academic Freedom In Our Time.* New York: Columbia University Press, 1955.

Mandel, William. *The Soviet Far East and Central Asia.* New York: Dial Press, 1944.

McKelvey, John J. *Handbook of the Law of Evidence.* St. Paul, Minn.: West Publishing Company, 1924.

Moore, Harriet L. *Soviet Far Eastern Policy.* Princeton, N.J.: Princeton University Press, 1945.

Morgenthau, Hans. *The Purpose of American Politics.* New York: Alfred A. Knopf, 1960.

Morris, Robert. *No Wonder We Are Losing.* New York: Bookmailer, 1958.

Morrow, William L. *Congressional Committees.* New York: Charles Scribner's Sons, 1969.

Packer, Herbert L. *Ex-Communist Witnesses: Four Studies in Fact Finding.* Stanford, Calif.: Stanford University Press, 1962.

Robinson, Edgar Eugene, and Paul Carroll Edwards, eds. *The Memoirs of Ray Lyman Wilbur.* Stanford, Calif.: Stanford University Press, 1960.

Rogin, Michael Paul. *The Intellectuals and McCarthy: The Radical Specter.* Cambridge, Mass.: M.I.T. Press, 1967.

Rosinger, Lawrence F. *China's Crisis.* New York : Alfred A. Knopf, 1945.

Rostow, Walt W. *The Prospects for Communist China.* New York: John Wiley and Sons, 1954.

Schaar, John H. *Loyalty in America.* Berkeley: University of California Press, 1957.

Service, John S. *The Amerasia Papers: Some Problems in the History of U.S.-China Relations.* Berkeley: Center for Chinese Studies, University of California, 1971.

Shannon, David A. *The Decline of American Communism; A History of the Communist Party of the United States since 1945.* New York: Harcourt, Brace, 1960.

Snow, Edgar. *Red Star Over China.* New York: Random House, 1938.

Steele, A. T. *The American People and China.* New York: McGraw-Hill, 1966.

Stormer, John A. *None Dare Call It Treason.* Florissant, Mo.: Liberty Bell Press, 1964.

Stouffer, Samuel. *Communism, Conformity, and Civil Liberties.* Garden City, N.Y.: Doubleday, 1955.

Tang, Peter S. H. *Communist China Today.* New York: Praeger, 1957.

Taylor, Telford. *Grand Inquest.* New York: Simon and Schuster, 1955.

Tsou, Tang. *America's Failure in China, 1941-50.* Chicago: University of Chicago Press, 1963.

Utley, Freda. *The China Story.* Chicago: Regnery, 1951.

Viereck, Peter. *Shame and Glory of the Intellectuals.* Boston: Beacon Press, 1953.

Watkins, Arthur U. *Enough Rope.* Englewood Cliffs, N.J.: Prentice-Hall, 1969.

Westerfield, H. Bradford. *Foreign Policy and Party Politics.* New Haven, Conn.: Yale University Press, 1955.

Weyl, Nathaniel. *The Story of Disloyalty and Betrayal in American History.* Washington, D.C.: Public Affairs Press, 1950.

White, Theodore, and Annalee Jacoby. *Thunder out of China.* New York: William Sloane Associates, 1946.

UNPUBLISHED MATERIALS

Carpenter, Thomas. "The Institute of Pacific Relations." Ph. D. dissertation, Fletcher School of Law and Diplomacy, Tufts University, 1968.

Condliffe, John. "The I.P.R." Personal manuscript.

———— "The Kyoto Conference." Personal manuscript.

Davis, George H. "The Dissolution of the Institute of Pacific Relations, 1944-1961." Ph.D. dissertation, University of Chicago, 1966.

Kohlberg, Alfred. "To My Grandchildren." Manuscript, 1958.

Martin, Ben Lee. "Interpretations of United States Policy toward the Chinese Communists, 1944-1968: Survey and Analysis." Ph.D. dissertation, Fletcher School of Law and Diplomacy, Tufts University, 1968.

McGlynn, Edna M. "The Institute of Pacific Relations." Ph.D. dissertation, Georgetown University, 1959.
Noble, Dorothy Louise. "The Institute of Pacific Relations." Master's thesis, Columbia University, 1934.
Oberdorfer, Donald, Jr. "The McCarran Committee's Investigation of the Institute of Pacific Relations." Senior thesis, Princeton University, 1952.

MANUSCRIPT COLLECTIONS

American Institute of Pacific Relations and Institute of Pacific Relations. Mss. Columbia University, New York. Contains IPR files mainly from 1925 to 1955. (Cited in footnotes as Columbia Files.)
American Institute of Pacific Relations and Institute of Pacific Relations. Mss. University of British Columbia, Vancouver, B.C., Canada. Papers contain IPR documents mainly from 1955 to 1960. Uncatalogued. (Cited in footnotes as Vancouver Files.)
Condliffe, John. Mss. Bancroft Library, University of California, Berkeley. Contains some correspondence about the IPR from one of its early staff members. (Cited in footnotes as Condliffe Papers.)
McLaughlin, Mrs. Alfred. Mss. Bancroft Library, University of California, Berkeley. Contains papers of a leader of the San Francisco IPR. (Cited in footnotes as McLaughlin Papers.)
San Francisco Bay Region IPR. Mss. Archives Section, Hoover Institution Library, Stanford University, Stanford, California. Contains files of the San Franciso IPR. Uncatalogued. (Cited in footnotes as Hoover Files.)

PUBLIC DOCUMENTS

State of California, Senate, Fact-Finding Committee of Un-American Activities. *Annual Report.* Vols. 3-5. 1947-49.
U.S.A. v. Owen Lattimore, U.S. Court of Appeals, District of Columbia Circuit, No. 111849, Brief for Appellee, 1953.
U.S.A. v. Owen Lattimore, U.S. Court of Appeals, District of Columbia Circuit, No. 121609, Brief of Appellee, 1954.
U.S.A. v. Owen Lattimore, U.S. District Court for the District of Columbia, No. 1879-52, Motion by Defendant to Dismiss the Indictment and Memorandum in Support of Motion, 1953.
Institute of Pacific Relations v. U.S.A., U.S. District Court, Southern District of New York, Decision of Court, March 31, 1960.
U.S., Congress, House of Representatives, Select Committee to Investigate Tax-Exempt Foundations and Comparable Organizations. *Hearings on Tax-Exempt Foundations.* 82d Cong., 2d sess., 1954.

————. *Report on Tax-Exempt Foundations.* Report No. 2681. 83d Cong., 2d sess., 1954.

U.S., Congress, Senate, Committee on Foreign Relations, Subcommittee Pursuant to S. Resolution 23. *Hearings on the State Department Employee Loyalty Investigation.* 3 vols. (pagination consecutive). 81st Cong., 2d sess., 1950. (Cited in the footnotes as *Tydings Hearings.*)

————. *Report on the State Department Employee Loyalty Investigation.* Report No. 2108. 81st Cong., 2d sess., 1950.

U.S., Congress, Senate, Committee on the Judiciary, Subcommittee on Internal Security. *The Amerasia Papers: A Clue to the Catastrophe of China.* 91st Cong., 1st sess., 1970.

————. *Hearings on the Institute of Pacific Relations.* 15 vols. (pagination consecutive). 82d Cong., 2d sess., 1951-52. (Cited in the footnotes as *McCarran Hearings.*)

U.S., Congress, Senate, Committee on the Judiciary. *Report on the Institute of Pacific Relations.* Report No. 2050. 82d Cong., 2d sess., 1952. (Cited in the footnotes as *McCarran Report.*)

NEWSPAPERS AND PERIODICALS

American Association of University Professors Bulletin. 1948-58.
Association for Asian Studies Newsletter. 1955-70.
Atlanta Constitution. October 1951; July 1952.
Bulletin of Concerned Asian Scholars. 1968-70.
Chicago Tribune. October 1951; July 1952.
China Monthly. 1939-50.
Christian Science Monitor. October 1951; July 1952.
Far Eastern Survey. 1932-61.
Journal of Asian Studies. 1941-60.
Los Angeles Times. October 1951; July 1952.
New York Herald-Tribune. October 1951; July 1952.
New York Times. 1950-56.
Pacific Affairs. 1928-60.
Plain Talk. 1946-50.
San Francisco Chronicle. October 1951; July 1952.
Seattle Post-Intelligencer. October 1951; July 1952.
Washington Post. October 1951; July 1952.

ARTICLES

Alsop, Joseph. "The Strange Case of Louis Budenz." *Atlantic Monthly*, 189 (April 1952): 29-33.
Black, Archie. "Millionaire Communist." *Plain Talk*, 3 (May 1949): 25-30.

Brogan, Dennis W. "The Illusion of American Omnipotence." *Harper's*, 205 (December 1952): 21-28.

Byse, Clark. "Teachers and the Fifth Amendment." *American Association of University Professors Bulletin*, 41 (Autumn 1955): 456-69.

Chafee, Zechariah, Jr. "Freedom and Fear." *American Association of University Professors Bulletin*, 35 (Autumn 1949): 397-433.

"The China Lobby." *Reporter*, 6 (April 15, 1952): 4-24, 5-24.

"Communist Threat Inside U.S." *U.S. News and World Report*; 31 (November 16, 1951): 24-30.

Deutscher, Isaac. "The Men Who Left Communism." *Reporter*, 2 (April 25, 1950): 4-8.

Fuchs, Ralph F. "Intellectual Freedom and the Educational Process." *American Association of University Professors Bulletin*, 42 (Autumn 1956): 471-81.

Gilbert, Brian. "New Light on the Lattimore Case." *New Republic*, 131 (December 27, 1954): 7-12.

Hinton, Harold C. "The Spotlight on Pacific Affairs." *Commonweal*, 56 (April 25, 1952): 65-66.

Huitt, Ralph K. "The Congressional Committee: A Case Study." *American Political Science Review*, 48 (June 1954): 340-65.

Hutchins, Robert M. "Are Our Teachers Afraid to Teach?" *American Association of University Professors Bulletin*, 40 (Summer 1954), 202-8.

Hyman Sidney. "Shall Senatorial Power Be Curbed?" *New York Times Magazine*, March 21, 1954, pp. 7, 28, 30, 32, 34.

Javits, Jacob K. "Some Queensberry Rules for Congressional Investigations." *Reporter*, 9 (September 1, 1953): 23-25.

Keating, Kenneth B. "Code for Congressional Inquiries." *New York Times Magazine*, April 5, 1953, pp. 10, 45-46.

Kohlberg, Alfred. "Owen Lattimore: Expert's Expert." *China Monthly*, 6 (October 1945): 10-12.

———. "Stupidity and/or Treason." *China Monthly*, 9 (June 1948): 151-52.

Kristol, Irving. "Ordeal by Mendacity." *Twentieth Century*, 152 (October 1952): 315-23.

Linebarger, Paul M.A. "Outside Pressures on China, 1945-1950." *Annals of the American Academy of Political and Social Science*, 277 (September 1951): 177-81.

Manley, Sheppard. "IPR: Carter's Pink Pills." *Plain Talk*, 1 (January 1947): 24-29.

———. "IPR: Tokyo Axis." *Plain Talk*, 1 (December 1946): 15-30.

Maxwell, Julian. "Frederick Vanderbilt Field." *American Mercury*, 75 (November 1952): 31-36.

Moyers, Bill. "Listening to America." *Harper's*, 241 (December 1970): 47-109.

Newsweek, 35 (May 15, 1950): 28-30.

Shannon, W. V. "Strange Case of Louis Budenz." *New Republic*, 125 (October 22, 1951): 9-10.

Steinberg, Alfred. "McCarran, Lone Wolf of the Senate." *Harper's Magazine*, 201 (November 1950): 89-95.

Thompson, Craig. "America's Millionaire Communist: Frederick Vanderbilt Field." *Saturday Evening Post*, 223 (September 9, 1950): 29.

Trow, Martin. "Small Businessmen, Political Tolerance, and Support for McCarthy." *American Journal of Sociology*, 64 (November 1958): 270-81.

Vital Speeches, 17 (April 15, 1951): 395-99.

Walker, Richard L. "Lattimore and the IPR." *New Leader*, 35 (March 31, 1952): S1-S16.

White, William S. "An Inquiry into Congressional Inquiries." *New York Times Magazine*, March 23, 1952, pp. 11, 25-27.

Williams, Richard L. "The Reds' Pet Blueblood." *Life*, 31 (July 23, 1951): 35-42.

Wriston, Henry M. "Fire Bell in the Night." *American Association of University Professors Bulletin*, 35 (Autumn 1949): 434-49.

PERSONAL INTERVIEWS

Barnes, Joseph. May 14, 1963.

Borg, Dorothy. May 9, 1963.

Buss, Claude. March 16, 1971.

Condliffe, John. April 14, 1970.

Fairbank, John K. May 1963.

Gerbode, Mrs. Frank. April 1970.

Heller, Mrs. Edward H. February 24, 1971.

Holland, William L. March 9, March 18, March 27, 1970.

Kohlberg, Laurence. January 22, 1970.

Lilienthal, Philip. July 8, 1970.

Lockwood, William W. March 26, 1963.

Martin, Charles. April 1970.

Morris, Robert. February 8, 1970.

Taylor, George E. April 1970.

Walker, Richard L. February 3, 1970.

Index

Acheson, Dean, 96
Agnew, Spiro, 172
Allen, James S., 20, 72, 101, 163
Alsberg, Carl, 24
Alsop, Joseph, 91
Amerasia, 23, 28, 29, 49-51, 148, 168
American Association of University Professors (AAUP), 120, 121
American Bureau for Medical Aid to China, 39
American China Policy Association, 49
American Committee for Chinese Industrial Cooperatives, 27
American Committee for Non-Participation in Japanese Aggression, 30
American Council, IPR: under Edward Carter's leadership, 14; and *Far Eastern Survey*, 22-25 *passim*; and Sino-Japanese War, 27; regionalism within, 30-33; and Kohlberg charges, 44; struggles against dissolution, 110-19; mentioned, 8, 9, 23, 34, 35, 160
American League against War and Fascism, 27
American Oriental Society, 128
American Peace Mobilization, 10, 33

American Russian Institute, 14, 28
Andrews, T. Coleman, 115, 116
Asia Society, 117
"Asiaticus" (Hans Mueller), 20, 22, 82, 83, 101, 114, 163
Association for Asian Studies, 130-34
Atherton, Frank, 3, 5, 7, 29

Ballantine, Joseph, 83
Barnes, Joseph, 12, 86
Barnes, Kathleen, 11, 88, 105
Barnett, Robert, 25
Barmine, Alexander, 85
Beebe, Lucius, 9
Bentley, Elizabeth, 65, 85
Bipartisanship, 47
Bisson, Thomas A., 24, 37, 51, 86, 157-58, 164-65
Bloch, Kurt, 104
Bogolepov, Igor, 85-86
Brandt, William, 19, 87
Browder, Earl, 28, 70, 71-72, 74, 83
Brownell, Lincoln C., 102
Buckley, William, 166-67, 168
Budenz, Louis: and Tydings Committee, 69-71, 158; and McCarran Committee, 85, 91, 114, 124, 125, 149, 150, 157; mentioned, 42, 152

183